I0417097

Texas Nature and Environmental Centers Guide

By Daniel W. Moulton, Ph.D.

Copyright © 2014 Daniel W. Moulton

TEXAS NATURE AND ENVIORMENTAL CENTERS GUIDE

by
Daniel W. Moulton, Ph.D.

No part of this book may be reproduced or utilized in any form
or by any means: electronic, mechanical or otherwise, including
photocopying, recording or by any informational storage and retrieval
system without permission in writing from the author.

Although the author has researched all sources to ensure the accuracy
and completeness of the information contained within this book,
no responsibility is assumed for errors, inaccuracies, omissions,
or inconsistency herein. Any mistakes are completely and totally
unintentional.

ISBN 978-1-4973-7124-8

Library of Congress Control Number:
2014933204

First Edition

Cover photo "Float trip on the Rio Grande"
Courtesy of Carol Cullar

Book design by MC2Graphics
www.mc2graphics.com

Published by Lone Star Productions
Contact: Ginnie Bivona
972-671-0002
ginniebivona@sbcglobal.net

This book is dedicated to the people who run and support the facilities and programs described in the book. Some of them do so at their own expense with limited external support. I hope this book can provide some measure of support to the promotion of their environmental agendas. The children they influence now will determine the nature of our society in the future.

Contents

About the Author xi

Introduction xiii

About This Guide xiv

Who Is This Guide For? xiv

How to Use This Guide....................................... xv

Acronyms/Terms Used in This Book xv

Outdoor Adventure Tips (Dos and Don'ts)...................... xvi

Introduction to the Natural Regions of Texas................... xvi

SOUTHERN HIGH PLAINS (The Panhandle)/ROLLING PLAINS 1

Southern High Plains 1

Rolling Plains 3

1 Alibates Flint Quarries National Monument 6

2 Wildcat Bluff Nature Center 8

3 Palo Duro Canyon State Park 10

4 Lubbock Lake National Historic Landmark 12

5 Sibley Nature Center 15

6 River Bend Nature Center 17

7 The Outdoor Education Center at YMCA Camp Grady Spruce 19

TRANS-PECOS (Mountains and Basins) 23

8 Franklin Mountains State Park.............................. 27

9 Centennial Museum & Chihuahuan Desert Gardens............... 29

10 Guadalupe Mountains National Park 31

11 Monahans Sandhills State Park 34

12 Chihuahuan Desert Nature Center 36

13 Barton Warnock Visitor Center 39

14 Big Bend National Park 41

EDWARDS PLATEAU/LLANO UPLIFT (Hill Country) **45**

15 San Angelo Nature Center 49

16 Fredericksburg Nature Center 51

17 Riverside Nature Center. 53

18 Cibolo Nature Center 56

19 Bear Springs Blossom Nature Preserve 58

20 Selah Bamberger Ranch Preserve 60

21 Westcave Outdoor Discovery Center. 64

22 Wild Basin Creative Research Center 66

23 Austin Nature and Science Center 68

24 Lady Bird Johnson Wildflower Center 71

25 Aquarena Center (Meadows Center for Water and the Environment) . . 73

26 San Marcos Nature Center. 75

OAK WOODS & PRAIRIES/BLACKLAND PRAIRIES **79**

27 Fossil Rim Wildlife Center 82

28 Fort Worth Nature Center & Refuge 84

29 Botanical Research Institute of Texas 86

30 Fort Worth Botanic Garden 88

31 Elm Fork Education Center 90

32 Bob Jones Nature Center & Preserve. 92

33 River Legacy Living Science Center. 94

34 Lewisville Lake Environmental Learning Area. 96

35 Collin County Adventure Camp. 98

36 Heard Natural Science Museum & Wildlife Sanctuary 100

37 City of Plano Environmental Education Center. 102

38 Blackland Prairie Raptor Center 104

39 Dallas Arboretum & Botanical Gardens 106

40 Perot Museum of Nature and Science 108

41 Texas Discovery Gardens at Fair Park. 109

42 Trinity River Audubon Center 111

43 Dogwood Canyon Audubon Center at Cedar Hill 113

44 Dallas ISD Environmental Education Center 115

45 John Bunker Sands Wetland Center. 117

46 Texas Freshwater Fisheries Center 119

47 Lake Waco Wetlands Research and Education Center. 122

48 McKinney Roughs Nature Park. 124

49 Mitchell Lake Audubon Center 126

PINEY WOODS 129

50 East Texas Ecological Education Center at Tyler (Nature Center) . . . 133

51 Caddo Lake State Park & Wildlife Management Area 135

52 Treetops-in-the-Forest 137

53 Jesse H. Jones Park & Nature Center. 140

54 Sheldon Lake State Park & Environmental Learning Center 143

55 Roy E. Larsen Sandyland Sanctuary 145

56 Big Thicket National Preserve. 147

57 Village Creek State Park 149

SOUTH TEXAS BRUSH COUNTRY 153

58 Rio Bravo Nature Center 156

59 Lamar Bruni Vergara Environmental Science Center 158

The World Birding Center. 160

60 Bentsen-Rio Grande Valley State Park 160

61 Quinta Mazatlan. 162

62 Santa Ana National Wildlife Refuge 164

63 Valley Nature Center 167

64 Estero Llano Grande State Park. 169

65 Resaca de la Palma State Park 171

66 Sabal Palm Sanctuary 173

GULF COAST PRAIRIES & MARSHES/COASTAL SAND PLAIN .. 177

67 South Padre Island Dolphin Research & Sea Life Nature Center 181

68 South Padre Island Birding and Nature Center 183

69 Laguna Atascosa National Wildlife Refuge. 185

70 Padre Island National Seashore 187

71 South Texas Botanical Gardens & Nature Center 189

72 University of Texas Marine Science Institute 192

73 Texas State Aquarium 194

74 Welder Wildlife Refuge 197

75 Aransas National Wildlife Refuge Complex 199

76 INVISTA Victoria ISD Wetlands. 201

77 Texas State Marine Education Center 203

78 Matagorda Bay Nature Park. 205

79 Matagorda County Birding Nature Center. 207

80 Texas Mid-Coast National Wildlife Refuge Complex 209

81 Sea Center Texas 212

82 Brazos Bend State Park 215

83 Kleb Woods Nature Center 218

84 Bayou Land Conservancy 220

85 Edith L. Moore Nature Sanctuary 221

86 Sims Bayou Urban Nature Center 223

87 The Children's Museum of Houston's EcoStation. 224

88 Hana & Arthur Ginzbarg Nature Discovery Center. 226

89 Houston Arboretum & Nature Center 228

90 Armand Bayou Nature Center 230

91 Eddie V. Gray Wetlands Education & Recreation Center 232

92 Baytown Nature Center 234

93 Artist Boat 236

94 Waterborne Education Center 239

95 Anahuac National Wildlife Refuge 241

96 Shangri La Botanical Gardens & Nature Center 244

References/Suggested Reading. 247

Appendix—An Environmental Primer 249

Human Population 249

Ecological Footprint 250

Global Warming & Climate Change. 250

Renewable Energy 251

Pollution & Toxic Chemicals 252

Endangered Species 252

The Economy vs. the Environment. 253

Politics and the Environment 254

Sustainable Life—The Big Picture. 254

About the Author

Daniel W. Moulton is a wildlife ecologist with a B.A. in biology (Colgate Univ., Hamilton, NY), a M.S. in wildlife ecology (Univ. of Wisconsin, Madison, WI), and a Ph.D. in wildlife science (Utah State Univ., Logan, UT). He was a postdoctoral research fellow at the Univ. of Minnesota in Minneapolis-St. Paul. He is recognized as a Certified Wildlife Biologist by the Wildlife Society.

He has worked for the U.S. Fish and Wildlife Service in Hawaii and Maryland, the Maryland Wildlife Administration in Annapolis, and for over 20 years at the Texas Parks and Wildlife Dept. in Austin. His work at TPWD focused on wetland ecosystems all over Texas, but especially coastal wetlands.

After retirement from TPWD, he taught for over six years as an adjunct professor of environmental science and biology at several colleges in the Dallas area.

He lives in Addison, Texas with his wife, Lynne, who is a professor of statistics at SMU, his daughter Claire, and his dog, Roxy.

Introduction

This guidebook is intended to encourage and facilitate visits to nature and environmental centers throughout Texas as well as promote environmental and ecological education.

All environmental problems facing us today—global, national, state, and local—ultimately result from our own values, attitudes, and behaviors. Many Americans, including a great many politicians, seem unaware of the inseparable connection between our economic health and the health of the ecological systems upon which we all depend. As Timothy E. Wirth, a former U.S. senator from Colorado put it, "The economy is a wholly-owned subsidiary of the environment."

A major problem with our increasingly urbanized population is a lack of understanding about our dependence on natural systems. People can't really care about things they don't understand. This growing disconnect doesn't bode well for our future. History re-enforces the fact that human societies must live in balance with natural systems. The natural laws we're ignoring determine how the planet functions; they can't be broken indefinitely without consequences.

Soon, we will have to abandon the use of coal and oil to generate energy and embrace renewable, sustainable energy sources. If we don't, global warming and climate change will make our children wish we had. We will need to lessen the impact our throwaway economy has on natural resource consumption and the creation of pollution and waste. If we don't, our grandchildren will wish we had. As the cartoon character Pogo Possum put it, "We have met the enemy, and he is us."

The root problem is one of education. It's knowledgeable, well-informed people, who are interested and engaged in conservation issues, who will have to help solve major environmental problems. If you want to find out more about environmental problems and potential solutions, please check out the appendix (An Environmental Primer). There, you can find the names and websites of some agencies and organizations that provide the most reliable environmental information available. Topics covered include population growth for Texas and the world, your own ecological footprint and how to make it smaller, pollution in your environment, global warming and climate change, and the environment vs. economic development.

About This Guide

The varied facilities and programs described in this guide are all about fighting "nature-deficit disorder" by educating while entertaining. The common thread is the opportunity for environmental education, and the majority of these facilities are located in or near large urban areas or other areas of dense population. Many rural areas have few or no such educational facilities and few kindred spirits struggling to find the local support needed to keep their programs viable. There are also several large cities, most notably San Antonio and El Paso, which seem to have a surprising lack of environmental education opportunities.

A number of public school districts operate their own environmental education programs and facilities; however, most of these programs are not open to the public or schools outside the home district. Only those ISDs that operate programs/facilities that are available to the public and/or schools outside the home district are described in this book.

All descriptions of facilities and programs have been reviewed and edited by the appropriate staff at the facilities. However, several programs that existed when I started the book are now defunct. Also, a few new ones have opened since that time. Therefore, I recommend that the reader check with the facility before visiting. If entrance to a facility or a specific program is free of charge, that's noted in the facility description. I haven't indicated entrance fees or other costs because they are subject to constant change.

Every facility teaches something about the major ecological region or system in which it is located. Most attempt to inform the visitor to some extent about the history, condition, problems, and projected future of the region.

While researching this book, I found some websites in need of updating and some too complex and time consuming to navigate. In some cases, a phone call produces the most reliable results.

All photos in the book are by the author unless otherwise noted. The figures are modified maps downloaded from the GIS Lab of the Texas Parks and Wildlife Dept.

Who Is This Guide For?

This guide is intended primarily for educators—schoolteachers, group leaders, and the most important educators of all: parents. Since children learn best when they're having fun, descriptions in this guide emphasize entertainment as well as education. The book can serve not only as a field and travel guide, but also as a library reference.

How to Use This Guide

This guide includes facilities in every major urban area of Texas, as well as those in more remote locations. Detailed information includes address, size, contact information, ecological description, programs, outreach programs, special features and amenities, directions, and GPS coordinates. Facilities are grouped within the 11 natural (ecological) regions and include locator maps with numbers keyed to the numbered descriptions.

Each natural region has a brief, nontechnical description of the major ecological system(s) found there. Photos of outstanding examples of regional ecosystems are featured in some cases.

Acronyms/Terms Used in This Book

ADA – The Americans with Disabilities Act of 1990: A federal law designed to protect handicapped people from various forms of discrimination. In this book, it pertains to the facility's accessibility to the handicapped. So, if a trail is ADA-compliant it's accessible to visitors in wheelchairs.

CPE – Continuing Professional Education credit for teachers: All certified CPE providers are approved and registered by the State Board for Educator Certification and the Texas Education Agency.

GLOBE – Global Learning and Observations to Benefit the Environment: A program that promotes worldwide hands-on primary and secondary school-based science and education. It promotes and supports students, teachers, and scientists in collaboration on inquiry-based investigations of the environment and the Earth system working in partnership with the National Aeronautics and Space Administration (NASA), National Oceanic and Atmospheric Administration (NOAA), and National Science Foundation (NSF).

GPS – Global Positioning System: A space-based satellite navigation system that provides location and time data in all weather if there is an unobstructed line of sight to four or more GPS satellites. The rapidly growing hobby called geocaching allows participants to use hand-held GPS units to hide and find caches of various objects and information.

LEED® – Leadership in Energy and Environmental Design: A suite of rating systems for the design, construction, and operation of high-performance green buildings, homes, and neighborhoods developed by the U.S. Green Building Council. Platinum status is the highest rating.

LRGV – Lower Rio Grande Valley: The LRGV extends from the town of Roma upstream to the city of Brownsville downstream. Most of the people and seven of the nine facilities in the South Texas Brush Country are in the LRGV.

Title 1 School – A school that is provided with funds from the U.S. Dept. of Education to pay for programs intended to bridge the academic gap between low-income and at-risk students and students in other local school districts.

VC – Visitor Center.

Outdoor Adventure Tips (Dos and Don'ts)

Dos

- Always check with facility personnel about things to see or avoid.
- Always take insect repellent just in case; ask if you need to protect against mosquitoes, ticks, or chiggers (redbugs).
- Protect yourself from the sun; wear a hat, sunglasses, and use a good sunscreen on all exposed skin.
- If you want to observe birds or other wildlife, binoculars and a field guide are needed. Many facilities provide bird lists and other guides.
- If you are going to hike any distance, wear proper hiking boots or shoes and make sure you carry ample water and a high-energy snack.
- Remember, kids who are improperly dressed, hot, hungry, thirsty, or fighting biting critters probably won't learn much.
- Take only pictures and leave behind only footprints.

Don'ts

- Never walk away from the marked trails (without prior approval).
- Never enter onto private property without landowner permission.
- Never harass or handle any wildlife, no matter how tempting.
- Don't remove anything, for example fossils or wildflowers. Other people want to see them too and almost all facilities prohibit removal of anything.
- Geocaches should not be established without prior approval of facility management.

Introduction to the Natural Regions of Texas

Texas is big, and is located in a region where a number of major life zones intersect and overlap. To the west are the arid deserts and high mountains, to the south is the sub-tropics, in the east are moist southeastern forests, and to the north the temperate Great Plains. And don't forget the 360 miles of Gulf coast. It's no wonder that Texas is so biologically and ecologically diverse.

Figure 1 shows 11 natural regions plus the Gulf of Mexico. The regions are delineated based on three interrelated factors: geologic history and the related soil types, climate (long-term temperature and precipitation averages and extremes), and regional ecosystems (plant and animal communities). The geology (types of bedrock and topography) of a region plays a major role in soil formation and topography can influence local weather and erosion patterns. Local climate influences soil formation processes through erosive forces breaking down bedrock and decomposing dead plant and animal matter. In turn, plant and animal communities influence the erosion of bedrock and soil formation processes and can even affect local climate.

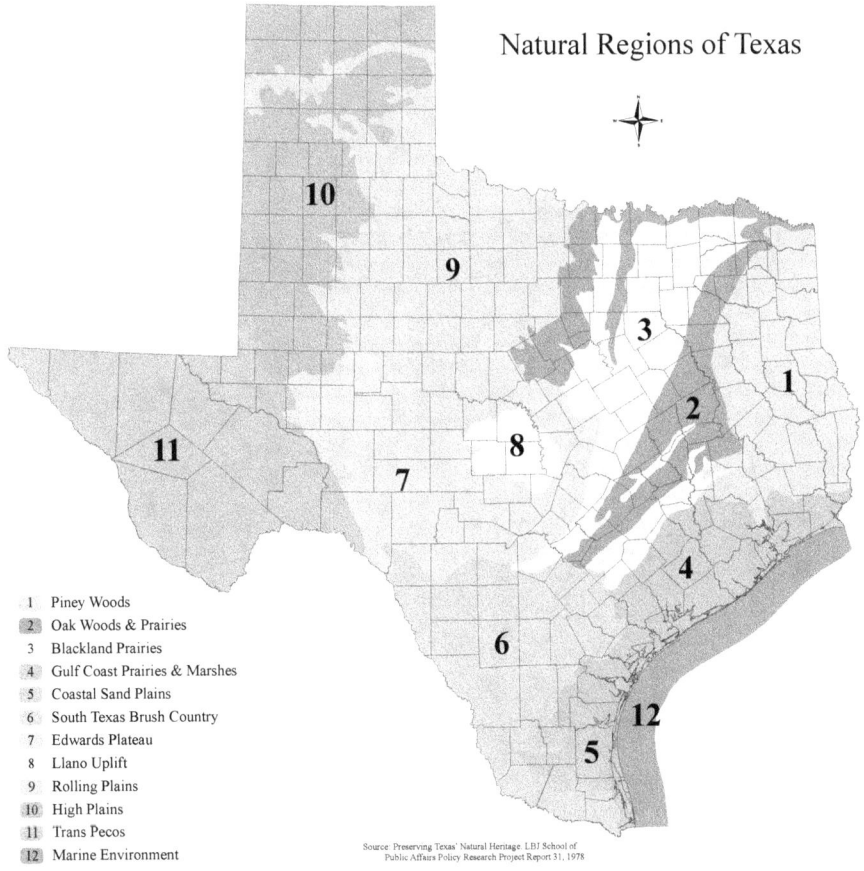

Natural Regions of Texas

1   Piney Woods
2   Oak Woods & Prairies
3   Blackland Prairies
4   Gulf Coast Prairies & Marshes
5   Coastal Sand Plains
6   South Texas Brush Country
7   Edwards Plateau
8   Llano Uplift
9   Rolling Plains
10   High Plains
11   Trans Pecos
12   Marine Environment

Source: Preserving Texas' Natural Heritage. LBJ School of
Public Affairs Policy Research Project Report 31, 1978

Figure 1—Natural regions of Texas

A major determinant of the plant and animal communities typical of a region is precipitation—both amount and seasonal distribution. Figure 2 shows average annual rainfall zones across Texas—from 56 inches in the cypress-tupelo swamps near Orange on the Sabine River to just 8 inches in the Chihuahuan Desert at El Paso. This variation is largely responsible for the great ecological diversity of Texas. If precipitation patterns change due to human-induced climate change, significant negative impacts to the ecological diversity of Texas will result.

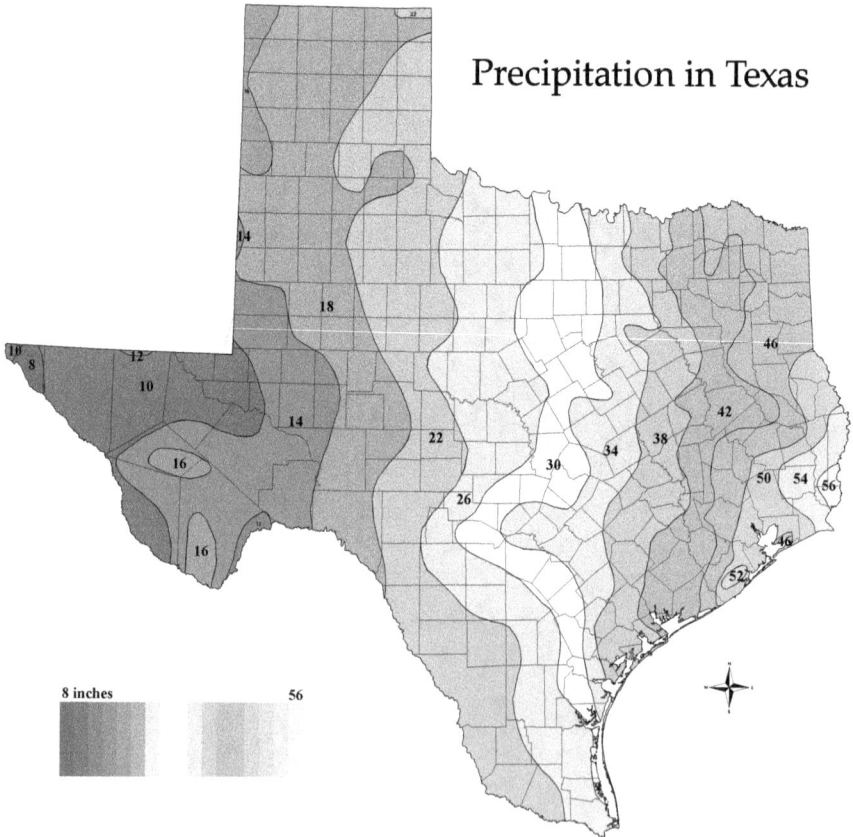

Figure 2—Rainfall zones in Texas

Since the arrival of Europeans, the impact of human population growth and human activities upon natural systems has been profound. Texas now has a population of about 26 million with projected growth to almost 36 million by 2040. All these people consume land, water, energy, and all other natural resources, producing environmental degradation. At the other end of consumption is the production of waste and pollution by the technologies that both create and ultimately dispose of the goods and services we consume. Some of this pollution comes back to us in the air we breathe, the water we drink, and the food we eat.

Land conversion to agriculture and commercial forestry plantations has gobbled up native prairies, forests, and wetlands. Now, urban and suburban sprawl are consuming prime farmland. Once farmland has been developed, it is very unlikely to return to the production of food and fiber. In the 1930s, Franklin D. Roosevelt said, "The nation that destroys its soil destroys itself." He was referring to the mismanagement of soil that led to the erosion and terrible dust storms of the Dust Bowl years. We would do well to heed his words today!

Overdrawing water from rivers and aquifers has caused groundwater levels to drop. This has resulted in many springs ceasing to flow and reduced flows in rivers, depriving floodplains and estuaries of needed freshwater inflows. It is certain that the demand for water by agriculture, industry, and cities and towns is going to cause water shortages in our future. What will happen then to our bays and estuaries, our rivers and streams, and our swamps and marshes? Water shortages will have very serious economic as well as ecological impacts. And yet, in most regions of Texas, water is so inexpensive that there is little reason for conservation. Benjamin Franklin once said, "We learn the value of water when the well runs dry." And so we will!

Overgrazing by livestock and the suppression of natural fires has allowed brush and many nonnative plants to invade grasslands, wetlands, and some forest types. Suburban sprawl results in smaller and smaller land holdings as large properties are subdivided and developed. This has caused the fragmentation of many habitat types and the decline of species that require large tracts of habitat and has favored the spread of many nonnative plants and animals that further threaten native species.

These extensive changes, and in some cases the economic implications, are discussed briefly in the description of each natural region. The people of Texas, whether or not they realize it, are dependent upon the ecological systems they live in.

SOUTHERN HIGH PLAINS (The Panhandle)/ROLLING PLAINS

Southern High Plains

The southern extension of the North American Great Plains has cold winters with minimum temperatures well below freezing and hot summers with maximum temperatures near 100 degrees Fahrenheit. Average annual precipitation varies from about 14 inches in the west to about 22 inches in the east. Strong winds blow much of the time and have helped Texas become the leading state in the production of clean, renewable wind-generated power. Elevations range from about 2,400 feet at Big Spring in the south and slope gradually upward to about 4,500 feet in the northwest near Dalhart.

The Texas High Plains are also known as the Llano Estacado. Legend holds that this means "staked plains" in Spanish and refers to the use of stakes to mark trails by the Spanish explorers. Darwin Spearing, in *Roadside Geology of Texas*, says the real interpretation is sensibly geologic, meaning "stockaded" or "palisaded" plains, which is how the edge of the plateau looks when viewed from below the caprock.

Around 10 million years ago, the Rocky Mountains north and west of Texas underwent uplift. Increased erosion of the mountains in wetter times spread a vast apron of gravel, sand, and clay eastward from the Rockies to as far as Dallas-Ft. Worth. These sediments, called the Ogallala formation, were deposited by rivers and streams eroding the Rockies from 10 to 4 million years ago. As the climate became drier, thick wind-blown deposits of sand and silt covered the older river deposits. Then, as the climate became more arid, much like today, caliche layers formed to cap the Ogallala formation. Caliche (ka-LEE-chee) is a white layer or crust of calcium carbonate (limestone), up to several feet thick, that forms in arid climates by evaporation of lime-charged groundwater from the soil surface. Topsoils range from clay hardpans in the north to sands in the south. The Ogallala formation contains water sands that hold the largest freshwater aquifer in the world, also called the Ogallala.

The last Ice Age, which began about 2 million years ago and ended about

10 thousand years ago, was a period of high rainfall. The Canadian, Red, Brazos, Colorado, and Pecos Rivers carried much more water than they do now. During this period, these rivers eroded the edge of the High Plains westward about 200 miles to its present position. The Canadian River cut a valley completely across the northern Panhandle and created the colorful "breaks" country. This valley is an extension of the Rolling Plains natural region.

Before the arrival of Europeans, the natural vegetation of the High Plains was shortgrass prairie dominated by blue grama, buffalo, and other grasses. Inhabitants of the prairie included black-tailed prairie dogs, black-footed ferrets, bison, pronghorn antelope, elk, gray wolves, grizzly bears, and mountain lions. Nearly 20 thousand playa lakes ("beach" in Spanish)—lakes that are round, shallow, and have no outlets—dot the regional landscape. They are important habitats for migrating and wintering waterfowl as well as many other animals and plants.

Today, most of the region is in agriculture. The Ogallala aquifer has been drawn down by pumping for irrigation faster than the aquifer can recharge, as have many playa lakes. Lowered water levels are causing a shift to more dryland farming, which is risky because it relies on rainfall. As water levels drop and energy costs rise, it becomes more costly to pump water for irrigation.

The region is known for its livestock feedlots, where animals are confined in very large numbers and fed grain to fatten them for market. This industry has caused water pollution problems in some areas.

Two important crops on the High Plains: cotton and wind

Rolling Plains

Below the eastern edge of the High Plains caprock is the escarpment breaks area of the western Rolling Plains. This is the transition zone between the Rolling and High Plains with the colorful canyons providing some of the most scenic landscapes in Texas. The Rolling Plains are also part of the southern end of the Great Plains.

Palo Duro Canyon, a geologist's dream

About 300 million years ago, the Ouachita Mountains were uplifted by the collision of continents, along what was then the southern margin of North America. This range ran from around Dallas-Ft. Worth, south to Waco, Austin, and San Antonio and west to Big Bend country. To the west of the mountains, the crust downwarped to form a deep basin called the Permian Basin. As the mountains eroded, the basin filled with sediments. The region was covered by shallow seas and sedimentary limestones, shales, and sandstones were deposited over most of West Texas. Deposits of bright red marine shales and sandstones formed in near-shore evaporation flats, as did salt and gypsum deposits. Marine organisms were the source of the famous oil deposits of the Permian Basin.

During the Cretaceous period (144 to 66 million years ago) Texas was again covered by shallow inland seas and thick beds of marine limestones formed over the older rocks. Along the shores of the inland sea, dinosaurs left their tracks in the Cretaceous muds. Dinosaur Valley State Park near Glen Rose is an outstanding example.

The Rolling Plains are sometimes called the "Red Bed" plains. As rivers eroded the edge of the High Plains westward 200 miles from Ft. Worth, starting about 2 million years ago, the older colorful rocks formed during the Permian were exposed. The valleys formed by the rivers and their tributaries are responsible for the rolling topography. The Red River gets its name from the red colored sediments it carries.

Average annual rainfall in the region varies from about 20 inches in the west to about 30 inches in the east, with peaks in the spring and fall. Elevations range from 800 to 3,000 feet. Summers are hot and dry with high evaporation rates. The region also has considerable wind resources that could be harnessed to generate clean, renewable power.

Historically, the region was mostly prairie with tall grasses in the east and mid-grasses in the west. Bluestems and gramas were typical. Under intense grazing pressure, short grasses like buffalo have increased. Grazing and suppression of natural wildfires have caused the invasion of brush like cedar (junipers), prickly pear, and especially mesquite, across the entire region. The region could now be characterized as a mesquite and short-grass savanna. Most of the region is in crop production and livestock grazing.

River floodplains in the north support trees like cottonwoods and in the south pecans and walnuts. Steep river valley slopes are dominated by cedars (junipers). Over-pumping of the Ogallala aquifer has reduced flows in the Canadian River and nonnative trees and shrubs have invaded floodplains.

Figure 3 shows the distribution of facilities in the High and Rolling Plains regions.

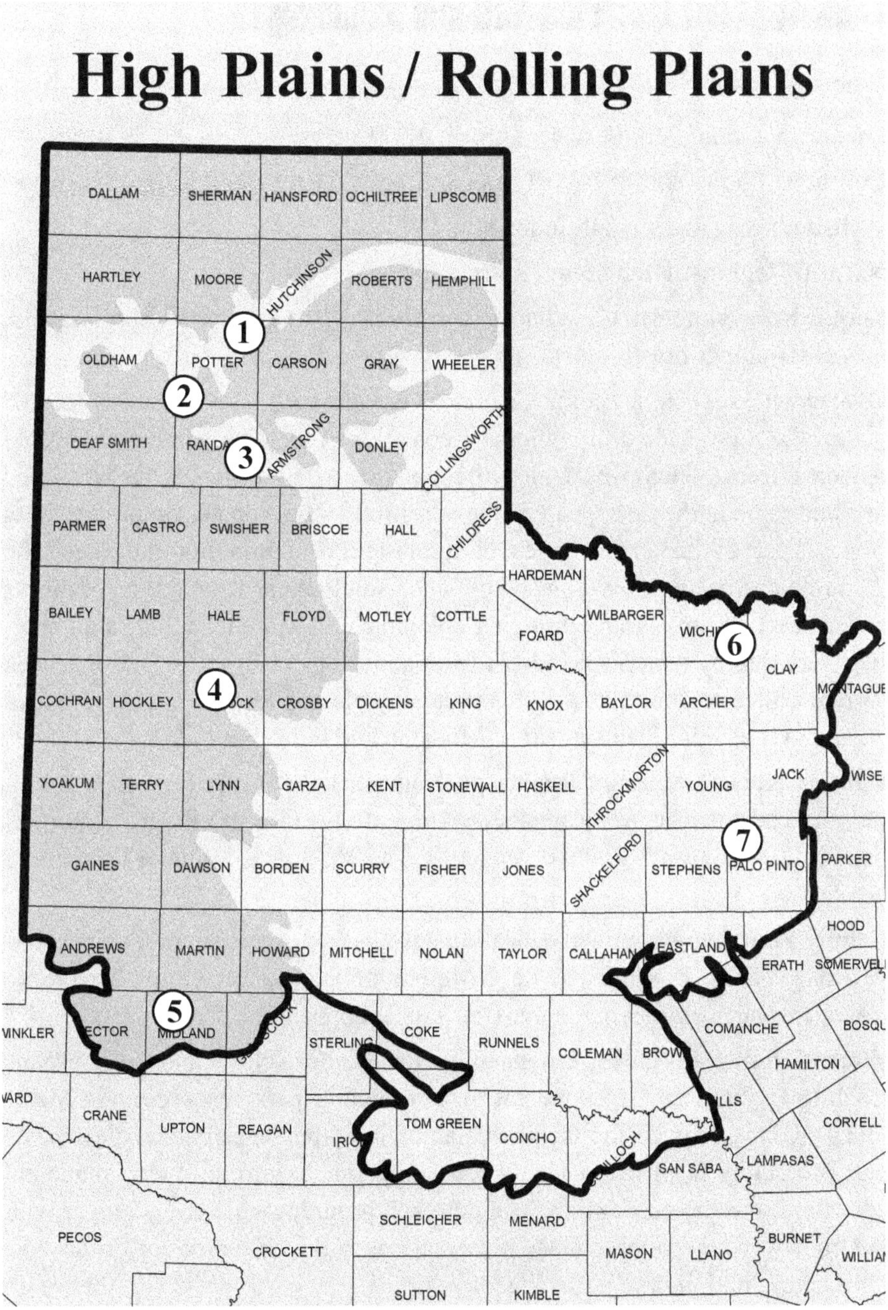

High Plains / Rolling Plains

Figure 3—Facilities in the High and Rolling Plains regions

Alibates Flint Quarries National Monument

419 E. Broadway, Fritch, TX 79036 (Administrative Office)

Owner: National Park Service   **Size:** 1,371 acres

Contacts: Phone 806-857-3151; Fax 806-857-2319; E-mail form on website

Website: www.nps.gov/alfl/index.htm

Natural Regions: High Plains/Rolling Plains

Major Ecosystem(s): Canadian River "breaks"; mesquite shrub/grassland; mesquite-juniper brush

Overview: This site is the only national monument in Texas, and is located within the Lake Meredith National Recreation Area. The name comes from Alibates Creek, which was named after cowboy Allen "Allie" Bates who lived in a line camp at the quarry site in the late 1800s. The Alibates dolomite (limestone) is part of the Permian-age Quartermaster Formation. In some places, the dolomite has been partly replaced by silica solutions to form a type of quartz called chert. "Flint" is dark or highly colored chert. More than 700 small quarries were dug by American Indians from about 1150 to 1450 AD. It has been surface collected for at least 13,000 years. Tools and arrowheads were traded all across the Great Plains as far as Montana and the Great Lakes.

Fun for Kids: The Junior Ranger program for kids of all ages offers activities and badges. The WebRangers program allows kids of all ages to participate online (www.nps.gov/webrangers/). The VC has exhibits, a film, and a bookstore.

Family Fun: Ranger-guided educational walks and quarry tours require reservations. The site is within the Lake Meredith National Recreation Area. Special events such as Junior Ranger Day and FlintFest are offered yearly.

Educational: Ranger-led, 2-hour guided walks for school and other groups teach kids about the environment and protecting park resources. A "Mammal Traveling Trunk" (the theme is mammals of the Texas Panhandle) can be checked out by local schools and is designed to help introduce environmental education into the curriculum. The outreach program will send a ranger with the trunk to your school to make presentations within 100 miles of Fritch, TX. Other presentations can be arranged.

Directions: Located 35 miles north of Amarillo. From I-40 in Amarillo, take the Lakeside exit north toward Lake Meredith NRA. Exit on TX 136 north toward Borger. Go 30 miles and turn west from TX 136 onto Cas Johnson Rd. Go 3 miles to the "Y" intersection and bear right. Go northwest 2 miles to the

Contact Station. The website includes a printable map.

GPS Coordinates: Latitude: 35°34.778`N     Longitude: 101°42.169`W

The Alibates Flint Quarries VC

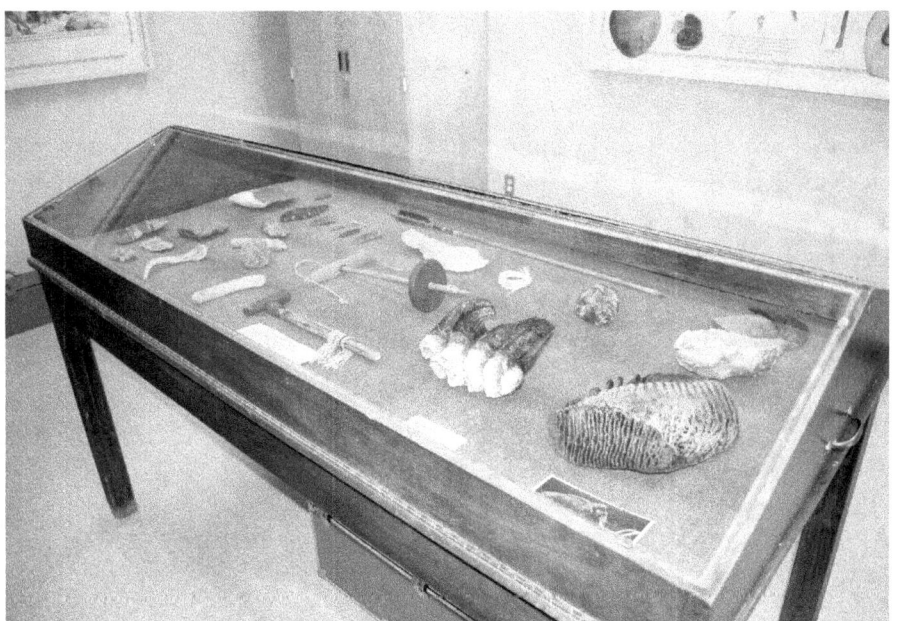

Alibates fossils and Native American artifacts

2 Wildcat Bluff Nature Center

2301 N. Soncy Rd., Amarillo, TX 79124

Owner: Wildcat Bluff NC   **Size:** 895 acres

Contacts: Phone 806-352-6007; E-mail info@wildcatbluff.org

Website: http://www.wildcatbluff.org/

Natural Region: High Plains

Major Ecosystem(s): Canadian River "breaks"; mesquite shrub/grassland

Overview: Wildcat Bluff was named by early cowboys on the historic Frying Pan Ranch for a den of bobcats that lived under the bluff. Wagon wheel ruts are still visible on the Gregg-Marcy Trail between Fort Smith, AR and Santa Fe, NM. The site consists of rolling short grass prairie invaded by mesquite, and riparian habitat, including large cottonwoods, along the valley of West Amarillo Creek, an extension of the Canadian River breaks. The bluff is part of the breaks that are the result of erosion by the Canadian River and its tributaries on the northern edge of the Llano Estacado.

WBNC is a research and educational facility that has become a regional attraction for students, scientists, and citizen scientists. Local colleges pursue ongoing research projects on the site.

Fun for Kids: All 5.5 miles of nature trails are open daily and have marked trail posts that correspond to booklets that emphasize Panhandle plants and animals or Native Americans and pioneers. LiBB's Trail is ADA-accessible and features an activity packet.

Family Fun: The Gilven Learning Center is used for periodic workshops and presentations dealing with ecology and sustainability issues in the Panhandle, as well as the peoples of the high plains. It also serves as a hands-on science learning lab.

Educational: Local grades 5–12 school groups conduct field trips at the center that can be guided by volunteers. School groups can observe local college research projects.

Directions: Located on the west side of Amarillo just south of the intersection of Highways 335 and 1061. WBNC is on Hwy 335 (N. Soncy Rd.) about 3 miles north of I-40. The website includes a printable map.

GPS Coordinates: Latitude: 35°14.112'N Longitude: 101°56.347' W

Wildcat Bluff Nature Center VC

Mounted exhibit of a bobcat, the Wildcat Bluff namesake

₃ Palo Duro Canyon State Park

11450 Park Rd. 5, Canyon, TX 79015

Owner: Texas Parks & Wildlife Dept.   **Size:** 29,182 acres

Contacts: Phone 806-488-2227; E-mail info@palodurocanyon.com

Website: www.palodurocanyon.com

Natural Regions: High Plains/Rolling Plains

Major Ecosystem(s): Mesquite-juniper brush; Prairie Dog Town Fork of the Red River

Overview: Palo duro is Spanish for "hard wood" and refers to the Rocky Mountain junipers, which were once abundant in the canyon. Palo Duro Canyon is known as the "Grand Canyon of Texas" and is the nation's second largest canyon at 120 miles long, up to 20 miles wide, and 800 to 1,000 feet deep.

The canyon rim is short grass prairie and the floor supports riparian habitat including tall grass, shrubs, and trees like cottonwood, mesquite, and several juniper species. The canyon was carved in the caprock during the last million years by an ancient river that began flowing when the Rocky Mountains uplifted. The Prairie Dog Town Fork of the Red River now flows through the canyon. The colors of the canyon come from layers of sandstone, claystone, and gypsum formations, some of which are 250 million years old. The Ogallala formation of sand, silt, clay, and limestone forms the hard caprock.

The park is the home of the Official Texas State Longhorn herd.

Fun for Kids: Old West Stables offers guided tours on horseback. There are hands-on children's nature programs and a Junior Naturalist program for ages 5–12. The play *Texas* in the Pioneer Amphitheater portrays pioneer life in the Panhandle (summer only).

Family Fun: The park offers a variety of family-oriented guided activities such as Texas Outdoor Family Workshops; family nature hikes; night hikes; seasonal interpretive talks; bird walks and talks; Native American presentations; and programs on geology, plants, animals, and history at the Lone Star Interpretive Theatre. The VC has a museum and store. The park features 30 miles of marked trails.

Educational: Guided bus tours for groups are available. For more info on educational programs, call 806-488-2227, ext. 226. A school outreach program is offered within a 50-mile radius of the park.

Directions: PDCSP is about 12 miles east of Canyon on SH 217. From Amarillo, take I-27 south to SH 217 and go east 8 miles to Park Rd. 5. The website includes a printable map.

GPS Coordinates: Latitude: 34° 59.092´N   Longitude: 101° 42.121´W

The Palo Duro Canyon State Park VC

A Barbary sheep diorama at Palo Duro Canyon State Park

The horseback riding center at Palo Duro Canyon State Park

Lubbock Lake National Historic Landmark

2401 Landmark Dr. Lubbock, TX 79415

Owner: Museum of Texas Tech Univ.   **Size:** 336 acres

Contacts: Phone 806-742-1116; Fax 806-742-2048; E-mail lubbock.lake@ttu.edu

Website: http://www.depts.ttu.edu/museumttu/lll/visitus.html

Natural Region: High Plains

Major Ecosystem(s): Yellowhouse Draw, an ancient tributary of the Brazos River

Overview: An archeological and natural history preserve, the Landmark contains evidence of 12,000 years of occupation by peoples on the Southern High Plains. There is no actual lake at the site. Ancient springs ceased flowing in the early 1930s. The site is in a meander of Yellowhouse Draw, an ancient tributary of the Brazos River. Active excavations go on in the summer. There are guided and self-guided tours, a learning and interpretive center, exhibitions, and programs for the public and for school classes and educators.

Fun for Kids: There are 4.5 miles of trails including a 3-mile nature walk. The Learning Center for kids and adults features stones, bones, plants, soils, etc. Summer classes for kids are available.

Family Fun: Public programs include annual festivals like Environmental Awareness Week, and special events such as Archeology in Action and Fall Fest of Cultural Heritage in October. Exhibition galleries feature the natural sciences and history. The Landmark Shop offers books and gifts.

Educational: School programs, both on and off-site, are aligned with state education standards. Programs include guided (for groups of 10 or more) and self-guided tours focused on archeology, geology, geography, and natural history. Teacher resources are available for these programs, and the staff can help teachers incorporate programs or visits into the regular curriculum. The Landmark is a certified CPE provider and offers professional development workshops and the Summer Educators' Academy.

Directions: Located on the northern edge of Lubbock at North Loop 289 and the Clovis Hwy (US 84) on Landmark Dr. Watch for signs on North Loop 289. The website has a printable map.

GPS Coordinates: Latitude: 33° 37.236´ N   Longitude: 101° 53.030´ W

The Lubbock Lake National Historic Landmark VC

Life-size mammoth replicas at Lubbock Lake NHL

A Native American diorama at Lubbock Lake NHL

Sibley Nature Center

1307 E. Wadley, Midland, TX 79705

Owner: Sibley Nature Center   **Size:** 49 acres

Contacts: Phone 432-684-6827; E-mail bwilliams@sibleynaturecenter.org

Website: www.sibleynaturecenter.org

Natural Region: High Plains

Major Ecosystem(s): Urban mesquite shrub/grassland, playas, and forest

Overview: SNC educates visitors about the natural and cultural history of the Llano Estacado. Programs presented by staff or cooperating organizations are given on-site and at schools, meeting rooms, ranches, and personal homes throughout the region. The center has a nature trail featuring native landscapes as well as displays and activities about regional habitats. The 5,200-sq.-ft. building includes a room for viewing the wildlife feeding station.

Other services include endangered species surveys of oil company leases, guided ranch tours promoted by owners, nature trail design and brochure writing for schools and landowners, schoolyard natural space planning, and plant/animal surveys for landowners.

SNC maintains the Midland County herbarium of wild plants and a non-lending research library. Staff answers phone and walk-in questions about the region. The center maintains a library of 50,000 photos and is working on producing smartphone apps for each of the 8 major habitats of the region. Drought-adapted plants can be purchased.

Fun for Kids: "Bug Camp" is a weeklong field and lab summer day camp for grades 4 6 that emphasizes the biology of insects and other arthropods. There are summer photography classes for kids (and also for adults) throughout the year.

Family Fun: The Permian Basin Outing Club and Sibley Camera Club offer year-round opportunities.

Educational: School programs are aligned with state education standards and are offered on-site or at the school or home school. The Texas Education Agency certified the center as an in-service provider of teacher training. The Sibley Academy offers a series of continuing education courses for adults in natural sciences, arts, history, and other special outdoor interests and activities. The website features virtual photo tours of the nature trail, photo essays of the 8 major habitats, photo essays of places to travel throughout the region, and over 1,000 essays about the history and ecology of the region.

Directions: Located in Hogan Park, just north of Wadley and about 0.5 mile east of N. Lamesa Rd. The website has a link (search for FAQs) to a printable map with driving directions.

GPS Coordinates: Latitude: 32° 01.996ˈ N   Longitude: 102° 04.239ˈ W

The Sibley Nature Center VC

The Sibley Nature Center wildlife viewing room

River Bend Nature Center

2200 Third St., Wichita Falls, TX 76301

Owner: RBNC   **Size:** 20 acres

Contacts: Phone 940-767-0843; Fax 940-322-1230; E-mail info@riverbend-naturecenter.org

Website: http://riverbendnaturecenter.wordpress.com

Natural Region: Rolling Plains

Major Ecosystem(s): Wichita River floodplain forests, wetlands, and ponds

Overview: RBNC is adjacent to the floodplain of the Wichita River. The nature trails are ADA-accessible (except for 1) and feature 17 acres of hardwood bottomland forests, ponds, and small wetlands on the floodplain. The 3-story high butterfly and nature conservatory emphasizes native plants and animals of the Rolling Plains. The conservatory includes an indoor pond with aquatic life and live prairie dog exhibit. The Bryant Edwards Learning Center includes live animal exhibits, seasonal exhibits, and a library with computers. United Children's Garden features a brook and pond, flowers, butterflies, birds, and more. Elizabeth Prothro Pavilion and J.S. Bridwell Terrace are available for picnics or rental for special occasions. There is a Nature Gift Shop.

Trained field guides are available to accompany visitors on tours.

Fun for Kids: Summer camps are offered for preschoolers through age 11. Live animal exhibits include prairie dogs and a Children's Garden with butterflies, birds, etc.

Family Fun: Specialty tours include Butterfly Days, Pioneer Days, and trail tours customized for the individual child or group. Special events include Nature Through Art, Earth Day, Bug Fest, Love of Nature Photo Contest, and ElectriCritters.

Educational: Guided nature trail programs offer a variety of themes for all ages and are available year-round. All curricula are aligned with state education standards. Eco-Kits are interactive environmental education programs presented in the school classroom (pre-K–6) by RBNC instructors.

Directions: From Hwy 277 (Seymour Hwy), take Sunset St. exit going north into Lucy Park. Before entering Lucy Park, turn left on Third St. and go up the hill. The website includes a printable map.

GPS Coordinates: Latitude: 33°54.720'N   Longitude: 98°30.805'W

The River Bend Nature Center VC and conservatory

River Bend live prairie dog habitat under repair

Peyton's Place memorial butterfly house at River Bend

The Outdoor Education Center at YMCA Camp Grady Spruce

3000 Park Rd. 36, Graford, TX 76449

Owner: YMCA of Metropolitan Dallas   **Size:** 865 acres

Contacts: Phone 214 319 9944; Fax 940-779-2939; E-mail website links

Website: www.ymcadallas.org/locations/camp_grady_spruce

Natural Region: Rolling Plains

Major Ecosystem(s): Possum Kingdom Lake on the Brazos River; hilly savanna of Ashe juniper and mesquite

Overview: Formerly mostly prairie, this region is now dominated by Ashe juniper (cedar) and mesquite. CGS is on a hill overlooking a bend in the Brazos River, now part of Possum Kingdom Lake, about 120 miles west of Dallas. Three separate summer camps serve younger boys (7–12 years), younger girls (7–12 years), and co-ed teens (13–16 years). The Outdoor Education Center operates year-round. The camp has the usual recreational facilities such as archery, boat docks, fishing, boating, etc.

The Man and the Environment Trail emphasizes human impacts on the local landscape and ecology.

Fun for Kids: Summer camps for boys 7–12, girls 7–12, and co-ed teens 13–16 include archery, fishing, boating, swimming, etc. Teen and challenge course programs are offered.

Family Fun: The Y Adventure Guide Program is for fathers and children from 3 years to grade 3. Family camping programs are available.

Educational: The Outdoor Education Center yearly instructs about 6,000 schoolchildren (grades 4–6) in various outdoor and environmental courses. Students spend a week at camp taking courses such as lake ecology, geology and fossils, erosion processes, prairie restoration and plant life, human impacts on the environment, etc. Students from over 90 schools and more than 30 districts are served. Courses are aligned with state education standards. Training for teachers, day camp staff, and safety skills is available.

Directions: From the DFW area, take I-20 west. Exit onto the Hwy 180 cutoff at Weatherford. Just west of Mineral Wells, turn north onto Hwy 337 and go 11 miles. At the 4-way stop in Graford, turn left onto Hwy 254 and go 8 miles to the intersection of Highways 254 and 16. Veer left onto Hwy 16, go 2 miles, and turn right onto Park Rd. 36. PR 36 will veer left after about 6 miles and dead end into Main and Ray Bean Camps. The website includes links to maps and driving directions.

GPS Coordinates: Latitude: 32°51.902ʹN   Longitude: 98°28.916ʹW

The Camp Grady Spruce general store

The Camp Grady Spruce education building

The Camp Grady Spruce boat dock, with Hell's Gate across the lake

TRANS-PECOS
(Mountains and Basins)

The Chihuahuan Desert of West Texas has the most complex geology and ecology of all Texas regions. The mountain ranges and plateaus, and intervening basins, are products of the earth's crustal plate being crunched and torn, volcanic eruptions, and the deposition of marine limestone reefs. And all the while, erosion has worn away the uplifted landscapes and deposited sediments into deep basins.

In the Franklin Mountains at El Paso and the Carrizo Mountains west of Van Horn, some of the oldest rocks in Texas—billion-year old Precambrian rocks—appear at the surface. The 300-million-year old Ouachita Mountain range, which is buried under sediments across most of Texas, comes to the surface in the Marathon uplift north of Big Bend National Park and in the Solitario dome west of the park in the Big Bend State Natural Area. As the Ouachita Mts. were uplifted, the adjacent crust warped downward to form the deep Delaware and Midland basins, which were covered by shallow seas. Sediments built up in the basins and limestone reefs grew around the edges of the basins. These Permian rocks can be seen in the Delaware, Apache, and Guadalupe Mts.

About 65 million years ago, the Rocky Mountains underwent a period of major uplift. All the northwest-southeast oriented mountain ranges of the region are part of this mountain building period. In the Big Bend, the older Ouachita range meets the younger Rockies to create a very complex landscape.

Around 35 million years ago, during a period of crustal cracking and fault formation, basins formed between the mountain ranges and volcanic magma rose to the surface. This was a period of volcanic eruptions that spread ash and lava over much of West Texas. Hills and knobs formed by volcanic intrusions add to the complex Big Bend scenery. Since then, erosion has been the dominant force acting upon the landscapes of West Texas. The talus slopes and outwash fans at the edge of every mountain and plateau attest to the relentless power of erosion and time.

All this geologic diversity is mirrored by great biological diversity. Plant communities include semi-desert grasslands; desert scrub typified by yuccas, creosote bush, tarbush, and lechuguilla; and mountain forests of oak, juniper, piñon and ponderosa pine, and Douglas fir. The mountain ranges receive more rainfall than the basins and plateaus and are called "sky islands" because of the greater biological diversity they support.

A much younger geologic feature of the region is the sand hills in the northeast where the Trans-Pecos meets the High Plains. This is a large area of active sand dunes that have been blown against the southwestern escarpment of the High Plains by strong westerly winds. The winds have to rise to get over the escarpment. As they rise, they lose velocity and drop sand that originates in the dry valley of the Pecos River to the west. Some dunes are stabilized by dwarf Havard shin oak. An excellent place to see the sand hills is Monahans Sandhills State Park.

Two major rivers form the southern (Rio Grande) and eastern (Pecos) borders of the region. The Rio Grande provides water for irrigated agriculture in the El Paso and Ciudad Juárez area. The river usually has no water flowing in it below El Paso until the Rio Conchos enters the Rio Grande from the south near Presidio, just above the Big Bend. If it were not for the Rio Conchos flows from Mexico, there would be no float trips through the magnificent canyons of the Big Bend. The Pecos also provides irrigation water for agriculture. The river floodplains were once dominated by cottonwoods and willows. Diminished flows have caused floodplains to be invaded by species of brush with deep taproots, especially nonnative saltcedar.

Elevations range from 2,500 to over 8,700 feet at Guadalupe Peak, part of a giant Permian reef, in Guadalupe Mts. National Park. Average annual rainfall varies from 8 inches in the west to 18 inches in the east, with July and August usually the wettest months. During the so-called "summer monsoon," thunderstorms form almost daily and can cause dangerous flash floods in canyons, draws, and arroyos. Soils in the region are as diverse as the geology and have formed from outwash sediments from the erosion of the mountains and plateaus.

Ranching (livestock grazing) has always been the basis of the economy in this region. Overgrazing of the fragile grasslands has caused soil erosion and a process called desertification. Semi-desert grasslands have been converted to desert scrub. If the timber of the "sky islands" were ever cut down, the biological diversity of the region would plummet. The ponderosa pine and southwestern white pine in the Guadalupe Mts. face a threat from expanding infestations of mountain pine beetles across western North America. This phenomenon appears to be related to warming temperatures brought about by climate change due to global warming.

Another regional environmental problem, one that might surprise you, is air pollution. Smoke from a large coal-fired power plant called Carbon II in Mexico at times degrades air quality and visibility at Big Bend National Park, and has also affected the McDonald Observatory in the Davis Mts.

Visibility problems due to air pollution in Big Bend National Park

Figure 4 shows the distribution of facilities in the Trans-Pecos region.

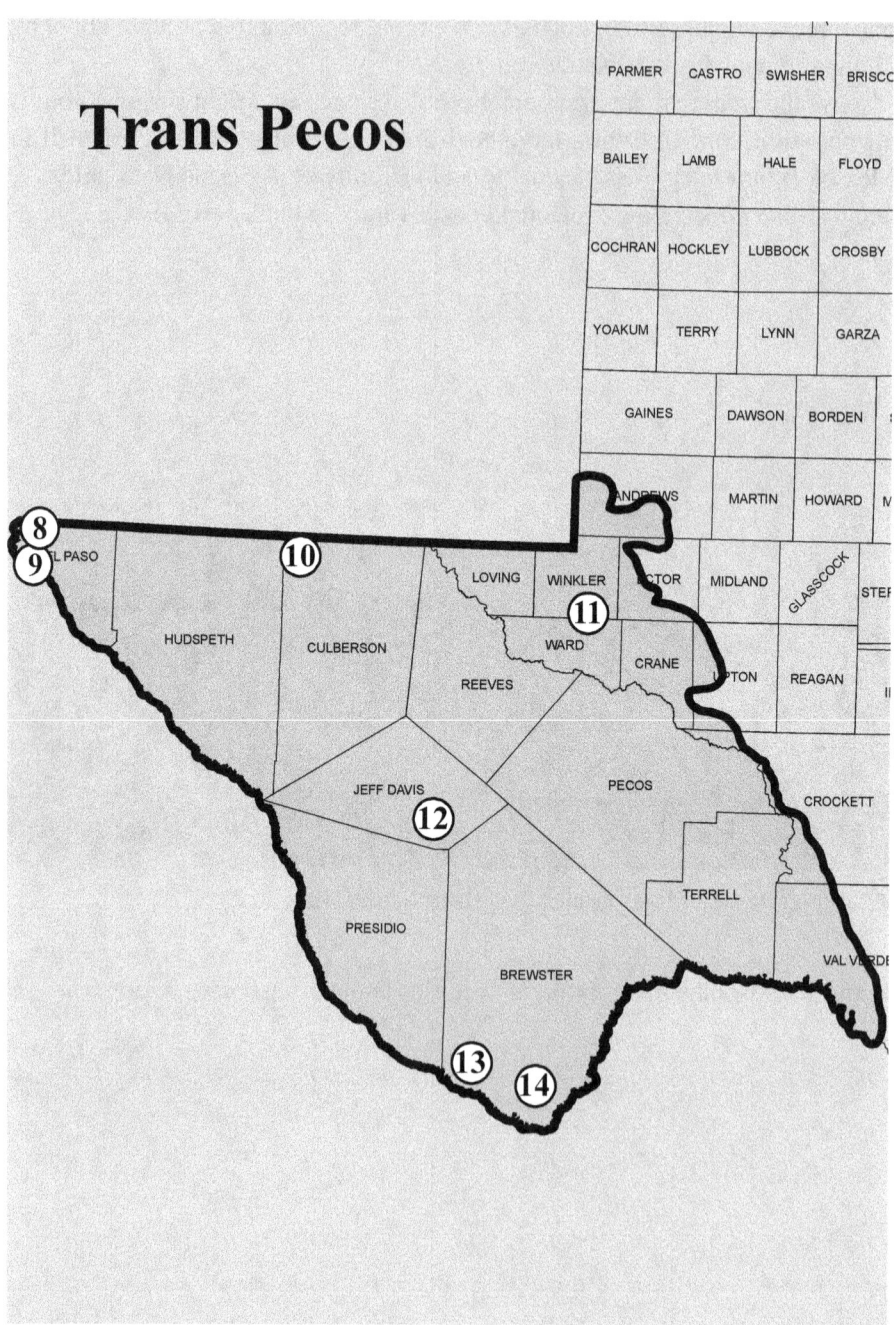

Figure 4—Facilities in the Trans-Pecos region

Franklin Mountains State Park

1331 McKelligon Canyon Rd., El Paso, TX 79930

Owner: Texas Parks & Wildlife Dept.   **Size:** 25,809 acres

Contacts: Phone 915-566-6441; Fax 915-566-1849

Website: http://www.tpwd.state.tx.us/state-parks/franklin-mountains

Natural Region: Trans-Pecos

Major Ecosystem(s): Chihuahuan Desert; Franklin Mts.

Overview: The Franklin Mountains overlook the Rio Grande and form the northern ramparts of the Paso del Norte (Pass of the North) leading from Mexico into the U.S. FMSP is entirely within the El Paso city limits and is the largest urban park in the nation. Plants and animals are typical of the northern Chihuahuan Desert. This is the only known location in Texas for a number of plant species, including the Southwest barrel cactus.

The Tom Mayes Unit of the park is a public day-use area and has an excellent wildlife viewing area at the bird blind. There is an extensive system of multi-use trails (over 100 miles), including horseback riding and mountain bike trails. There is a designated paraglider launch area.

The Wyler Aerial Tramway is the only publicly accessible cable car ride in Texas. It is located at a different address and is run separately from FMSP.

Fun for Kids: The Junior Ranger Program is a self-paced course of activities designed to teach kids about the park and good stewardship of the park and its resources. The Wyler Aerial Tramway cable car ride is located nearby.

Family Fun: Summer night hikes include topics such as astronomy and nocturnal animals and sounds. Over 100 miles of hiking, horseback riding and mountain biking trails. The Chihuahuan Desert Fiesta is held every September. This includes free tours and demonstrations by educators on desert plants and animals; entry fees are waived for this event.

Educational: FMSP conducts public guided nature tours on easy, moderate, and difficult trails. These ranger-led tours are conducted on the first and third weekends of the month. Special arrangements can be made for school and other group tours. FMSP is home to one of the U.S.'s only tin mining and smelting operations. Tours into the old abandoned mines are conducted throughout the year.

Directions: FMSP is on the northern edge of El Paso and has 3 primary access points. Take I-10 west following the Rio Grande to the Canutillo/Trans-Mountain Rd. exit. Turn east toward the mountains and go about 4 miles east of I-10

or take Loop 375/Trans-Mountain Rd. going west up and over the Franklin Mts. The park entrance is 3 miles down from the summit. On the east side of the mountains and from Hwy 54, exit on Fred Wilson Rd. and turn west toward the mountains.

GPS Coordinates (Tom Mays Unit): Latitude: 31° 54.466 N   Longitude: 106° 31.549 W

Franklin Mountains State Park VC

The Wyler Aerial Tramway

Centennial Museum & Chihuahuan Desert Gardens

500 West University Ave., El Paso, TX 79968

Owner: The University of Texas at El Paso

Contacts: Phone 915-747-5565; Fax 915-747-5411; E-mail museum@utep.edu

Website: http://museum.utep.edu/

Natural Region: Trans-Pecos

Major Ecosystem(s): Chihuahuan Desert (urban gardens)

Overview: The museum's permanent exhibits and temporary galleries focus on the natural and cultural history of the Chihuahuan Desert region, the largest desert in North America. Over 600 species of native plants from the Greater Chihuahuan Desert region are grown in the Desert Gardens.

There is no entry fee for the museum or gardens.

Fun for Kids: School tours of the Desert Gardens or museum can be scheduled. The museum has a gift shop.

Family Fun: Activities for both children and adults include FloraFest, featuring native plant presentations and sales, and SunScape native plant gardening instruction.

Educational: An online course about the Chihuahuan Desert is offered. The Desert Diary online lesson plans are expanded versions of the KTEP public radio daily presentations about the Chihuahuan Desert region's natural and cultural history. The Chihuahuan Desert Teaching Module is one of several web-based natural history courses available on the museum's website.

Directions: The museum and gardens are located at the corner of University and Wiggins on the UTEP campus. The elevator entrance is off Univ. Ave. The campus is accessed from I-10 at the UTEP/Shuster exit and can also be accessed via Univ. Ave. from Mesa St. The website includes a printable map.

GPS Coordinates: Latitude: 31° 46.165' N   Longitude: 106° 30.374' W

The Univ. of Texas El Paso Centennial Museum

Chihuahuan Desert Gardens at the Centennial Museum

Mounted animal exhibits in the Centennial Museum

Guadalupe Mountains National Park

400 Pine Canyon Dr., Salt Flat, TX 79847

Owner: National Park Service   **Size:** 86,416 acres

Contacts: Phone 915-828-3251; Fax 915-828-3269; E-mail form on website

Website: www.nps.gov/gumo/index.htm

Natural Region: Trans-Pecos

Major Ecosystem(s): Chihuahuan Desert; Guadalupe Mts.

Overview: GMNP protects world-class geologic resources including one of the world's best examples of a fossilized marine sponge and coral reef. The reef formed during the Permian period about 260 million years ago when the region was covered by an arm of the tropical Permian ocean called the Delaware Sea.

About 26 million years ago, faulting and uplift raised the Capitan Reef almost two miles. Erosion has worn away the softer sediment layers and left behind the harder limestone reef. The park has great biodiversity because of altitudinal zonation (3,689–8,749 feet) and convergence of species typical of the Rocky Mts., Great Plains, and Chihuahuan Desert. At the highest elevations are coniferous forests of Douglas fir, ponderosa pine, and southwestern white pine.

GMNP contains 7 of the 10 highest peaks in Texas, including 8,749-foot

Guadalupe Peak (the highest point in Texas), and the second largest gypsum dune field in the U.S.

Fun for Kids: Jr. Paleontologist, Jr. Ranger, Sr. Ranger, and Jr. Wilderness Ranger programs are offered. The annual Jr. Ranger Day is held every April. Boy & Girl Scout awards/patch programs are offered.

Family Fun: Special activities, talks, guided hikes, and evening programs are offered throughout the year. There are 80 miles of hiking trails (60 percent open to equestrian use). There are 3 self-guided nature trails located at the VC, McKittrick Canyon, and Dog Canyon. The McKittrick Canyon Contact Station has exhibits and a push-button audio-visual program. There are campgrounds at Pine Springs and Dog Canyon. Group campsites are available by reservation up to 60 days in advance.

Educational: The entrance fee is waived for groups if the purpose of the visit is educational (at least two weeks advance notice required). GMNP is an outstanding geological and biological natural classroom. The Pine Springs VC has a variety of exhibits and a touch-screen "electronic ranger" that presents information about the geology, natural, and cultural history of the park. There is also a 12-minute orientation slide show.

Directions: On US Hwy 62/180, 110 miles east of El Paso, 65 miles north of Van Horn, TX, and 56 miles southwest of Carlsbad, NM. The Pine Springs VC is on US 62/180, 9 miles north of the junction with TX 54. The website includes printable brochures with park and area maps.

GPS Coordinates: Latitude: 31° 53.545´N   Longitude: 104° 49.240´W

Chihuahuan Desert wildlife diorama in the VC

The Guadalupe Mts. from the south

Guadalupe Mts. National Park VC

Monahans Sandhills State Park

Box 1738, Monahans, TX 79756

Owner: Texas Parks & Wildlife Dept.   **Size:** 3,840 acres

Contacts: Phone 432-943-2092

Website: http://www.tpwd.state.tx.us/state-parks/monahans-sandhills

Natural Region: Trans-Pecos

Major Ecosystem(s): Wind-blown sand dunes; Havard shin oak brush

Overview: MSSP is a small part of a dune field that is about 200 miles long, extending from south of Monahans into New Mexico. Most of the dunes are stabilized by vegetation such as Havard shin oak brush, but the park is in an area where many dunes are not stabilized and are still actively changing size and shape in response to prevailing winds. The sands have been blown from the dry Pecos River valley to the west over the last one million years and dropped at the foot of the High Plains escarpment.

The VC is ADA-compliant and has a park store.

Fun for Kids: Sand surfing on the dunes is popular, and sand toboggans and disks can be rented. Scenic windows permit viewing of birds and other wildlife as they come to food and watering stations.

Family Fun: There is a 0.25-mile, self-guided nature trail at the VC. There is an equestrian day-use area (additional fees required).

Educational: The Dunagan VC has hands-on exhibits of the cultural heritage and natural history of the sandhills, including dune dynamics, Permian Basin heritage, and wildlife habitat. A park orientation talk is available. There is a reduced entrance fee for school-sponsored trips with prior approval.

Directions: MSSP is about a 30-minute (30 miles) drive west of Odessa on I-20. Exit at mile marker 86 to Park Rd. 41. The website includes a printable map. Directions provided by GPS units are inaccurate for this location and should be avoided when traveling to MSSP.

Monahans Sandhills State Park entrance and VC

Monahans Sandhills State Park VC

Active sand dunes at Monahans Sandhills State Park

12 Chihuahuan Desert Nature Center

43869 SH 118, Fort Davis, TX 79734

Owner: Chihuahuan Desert Research Institute   **Size:** 507 acres

Contacts: Phone 432-364-2499; Fax 432-364-2686; E-mail choyt@cdri.org

Website: www.cdri.org

Natural Region: Trans-Pecos

Major Ecosystem(s): Chihuahuan Desert; foothills of the Davis Mountains

Overview: The VC features interpretive exhibits, a wildscape demonstration garden with 67 species of wildlife-attracting native plants, and a geological timeline constructed of rock samples from the region. The Chihuahuan Desert Mining Heritage Exhibit interprets the mining history of the area. Our Dynamic Landscape, an exhibit on the highest point of the property, relates culture and history to the geology of the region. A self-guided walking tour takes you through the 20-acre botanical gardens to the cactus and succulent greenhouse. Over 165 species of trees, shrubs, and forbs are featured in the gardens. The greenhouse preserves over 200 species of Chihuahuan Desert cacti.

Fun for Kids: Summer nature day camps are offered for ages 4–10. The VC features the Leapin' Lizards Nature Shop. *The Desert NewsFlash* free e-mail newsletter is available.

Family Fun: Family activities like the Desert Scavenger Hunt and the Desert After Dark are offered. Over three miles of trails start at the VC. A trail guide brochure is available.

Educational: CDRI has a wide variety of educational programs including in-school visits by staff and outdoor education programs aligned with state education standards. Life-long learning programs and special events include lectures, workshops, guided hikes and walks, field trips, day camps for kids, etc. Teachers' workshops for CPE credit are offered occasionally. The Earth Rocks!!! is a celebration of National Earth Science Week, and limited student scholarships are made available. The Earth Rocks!!! in October and Bug Day in May are limited to school groups only and not open to the general public.

Directions: CDRI is about 5 miles south of Fort Davis on SH 118. The website includes a printable map.

GPS Coordinates: Latitude: 30° 32.483´ N   Longitude: 103° 51.053´ W

The Chihuahuan Desert Nature Center south of Ft. Davis

Chihuahuan Desert Research Institute's cactus and succulent greenhouse

The Chihuahuan Desert Nature Center's mining heritage exhibit

Barton Warnock Visitor Center

HC 70, Box 375, Terlingua, TX 79852

Owner: Texas Parks & Wildlife Dept.   **Size:** 99.9 acres

Contacts: Phone 432-424-3327

Website: http://www.tpwd.state.tx.us/state-parks/barton-warnock

Natural Region: Trans-Pecos

Major Ecosystem(s): Chihuahuan Desert; Rio Grande

Overview: Located in Brewster County, BWVC serves as the eastern entrance to Big Bend Ranch State Park and interprets 570 million years of geological history and the ecology of the Chihuahuan Desert and the Rio Grande. It presents an archeological, historical, and natural history profile of the Big Bend region. The Interpretive Center "Una Tierra – One Land" is the product of an international partnership, and most information, including captions and text, is presented in both English and Spanish.

The bookstore includes titles of regional interest.

Fun for Kids: The Interpretive Center is self-guiding, but interpreted guided tours for groups can be arranged. There is a bookstore and gift shop.

Family Fun: The self-guided 2.5-acre botanical garden features the characteristic plants of the Chihuahuan Desert. Guided tours of the garden are by reservation only.

Educational: There is a reduced entrance fee for school-sponsored trips. The Interpretive Center includes geological and archeological artifact displays, a research library, and an auditorium for educational classes and special events.

Directions: Located 1 mile east of Lajitas on FM 170.

GPS Coordinates: Latitude: 29° 16.213' N   Longitude: 103° 45.432' W

From the trail behind the Barton Warnock VC

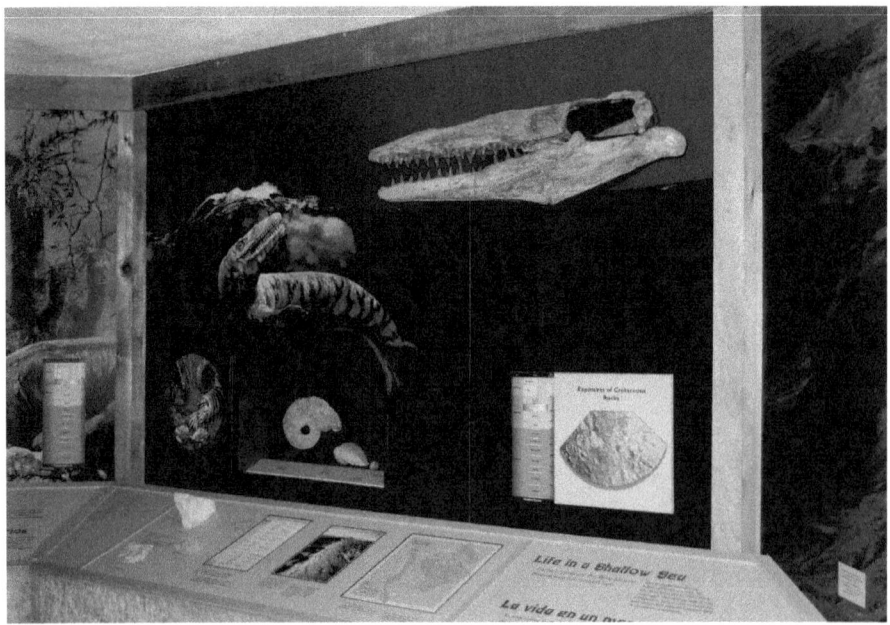

Bilingual fossil exhibit in the Barton Warnock VC

Big Bend National Park

P.O. Box 129, Big Bend NP, TX 79834

Owner: National Park Service   **Size:** 801,163 acres

Contacts: Phone 432-477-2251; Fax 432-477-1176; E-mail form on website

Website: www.nps.gov/bibe/

Natural Region: Trans-Pecos

Major Ecosystem(s): Chihuahuan Desert; Chisos Mts.; Rio Grande

Overview: The region is named for the abrupt change in the direction of flow (the Big Bend) in the Rio Grande. BBNP is the largest protected area of Chihuahuan Desert in the U.S., and boasts more types of birds, bats, reptiles, and cacti than any other national park in the U.S. The biological diversity is due to the many habitats of the desert, river, and different mountain life zones. The park also protects world class geological, paleontological (fossil), and cultural resources.

The 118 miles of river that form the park's southern boundary include the spectacular canyons of Santa Elena, Mariscal, and Boquillas.

Fun for Kids: There is a Junior Ranger program for young children. The Rio Grande Village nature trail has a boardwalk on a beaver pond. There are bookstores at all 5 VCs and an online bookstore (http://www.bigbendbookstore.org/).

Family Fun: BBNP has five VCs all of which have exhibits, nature trails, daily ranger-led activities, and evening programs. Ranger-led programs include guided hikes, slide programs, bird walks, workshops, and guided tours of various park features. Group campsites require reservations. Single and multi-day commercial river float trips are available.

Educational: The "Parks as Classrooms" program provides state-aligned curriculum materials for teachers including biodiversity, cultural history, and geology in English and Spanish. The website includes pages to assist teachers and group leaders in planning field trips. The entrance fee is waived for educational groups visiting the park as part of their course work.

Directions: There are several highways leading to BBNP. Take TX 118 from Alpine to Study Butte, or FM 170 from Presidio to Study Butte, then 26 miles east to park headquarters. Or, take US 90 or US 385 to Marathon, then 70 miles south to park headquarters. The website includes detailed printable maps.

GPS Coordinates: Latitude: 29° 19.696ʹN   Longitude: 103° 12.374ʹW

The Panther Junction VC in Big Bend National Park

Rio Grande Village nature trail and boardwalk in Big Bend National Park

The Rio Grande near Boquillas Canyon in Big Bend National Park

EDWARDS PLATEAU/LLANO UPLIFT
(Hill Country)

During the Cretaceous period 100 million years ago, all of Central Texas was under an ocean. Thick marine limestone and other sedimentary rocks were laid down over the entire region. From 20 to 10 million years ago, Central Texas was elevated 2,000 feet without deformation of the Cretaceous rocks. This limestone bench is the Edwards Plateau. To the east and south of the bench, along the fault zone where the plateau was uplifted, is a steep fault face called the Balcones escarpment. Balcones is Spanish for "balcony," a good analogy for the appearance of the escarpment.

For the last 10 million years, erosion by rivers and streams has carved away at the southern and eastern margins of the plateau. The west half of Central Texas is still a high, flat plateau, but the east half, the Hill Country, is deeply eroded and well drained by rivers.

The region is renowned for its limestone karst (caves) habitats. Even unpolluted rainwater is slightly acidic because carbon dioxide from the air dissolves in the water to form carbonic acid—the same weak acid that's in your carbonated soft drink. The weakly acidic groundwater slowly dissolves away limestone, forming caves and underground rivers such as the Edwards Aquifer. The Edwards Aquifer provides all of San Antonio's water as it does for much of the Hill Country. It also feeds the famous springs that pour out from the faults at the edge of the plateau, for example, Barton Springs in Austin, San Marcos Springs, and Comal Springs in New Braunfels. San Marcos and Comal Springs are the largest in the southwestern U.S. and are the sources of the San Marcos and Comal Rivers. Many other rivers, including the Devil's, Nueces, Frio, Medina, San Antonio, Guadalupe, Pedernales, Llano, and San Saba have their headwaters on the Edwards Plateau. On the plateau, they run clear and clean and the narrow floodplains support gallery forests of baldcypress, sycamore, sugarberry, pecan, ash, and cottonwood. The springs and caves of the Edwards Aquifer are home to many rare and endangered fish, amphibians, and invertebrates. Large colonies of Mexican free-tailed bats summer in some of the caves. A large number of Mexican free-tails summer under the Congress

Avenue bridge in Austin and have become a major attraction for both tourists and residents.

The Llano Uplift, although surrounded by the Hill Country, has much more ancient origins. The Llano rocks, at 1.35 billion years old, are probably the oldest surface rocks in Texas. At one time, central Texas was in an ocean basin off the coast of North America. When North America collided with another continent approximately one billion years ago, the collision zone caused a mountain range to be uplifted and allowed hot magma to rise to the surface to form granite. Over the next 400 million years, erosion wore down the mountains and the two continents drifted apart. Again, the region was covered by the sea. During the Paleozoic era (600 to 300 million years ago), marine sediments covered the old worn down mountain range. Then, 300 million years ago, another collision of continents created the Ouachita Mountains. This range was eroded flat, the continents again separated, and the Gulf of Mexico began to open about 200 million years ago. Central Texas was again under the ocean and Cretaceous marine sediments (the Edwards Plateau) were laid over the eroded surface of the ancient rocks. Then the Edwards Plateau was uplifted along with the underlying ancient Llano rocks. Over the last 10 million years, the erosion of the plateau limestone has created the Hill Country and exposed the ancient granite and metamorphic rocks (gneiss and schist) of the Llano Uplift. Enchanted Rock, north of Fredericksburg, is the second largest granite dome in the U.S. after Stone Mountain, Georgia.

Rainfall over the region varies from 15 inches in the west to 34 inches in the east and is highest in the spring and early fall. Elevations range from about 825 to 3,000 feet. Soils in the Hill Country are usually shallow due to soil erosion and alkaline because of the limestone bedrock. Soils of the Llano Uplift are sandy and formed from the weathering of granite.

Today, the vegetation of the region is oak-juniper (cedar) woodlands, plateau live oak savanna, mesquite-mixed brush savanna, and some grasslands. Grasslands and savannas were more common in the past. Ashe juniper (cedar) has spread widely due to overgrazing, suppression of wildfire, and soil erosion. Heavy use of Edwards Aquifer water has resulted in diminished flows in many springs and rivers and is threatening some of the rare and endangered species dependent upon the aquifer. The lowered water table also threatens people, as many wells have gone dry and water shortages seem inevitable for this region. Endangered golden-cheeked warblers and black-capped vireos nest only in the Ashe juniper-oak woodlands of the region.

Livestock grazing is the primary land use in the region but hunting of white-tailed deer and a host of imported exotic ungulates is an important source of income for many landowners. There has been tremendous population growth of cities along the Balcones Fault zone from San Antonio to north of Austin. This urbanization is spreading relentlessly into the Hill Country. The region has also become a popular retirement destination. The steadily decreasing size of the average land holding is fragmenting and degrading the natural habitats of the region.

Hill Country habitat encroachments west of Austin

Figure 5 shows the distribution of facilities in the Edwards Plateau and Llano Uplift regions.

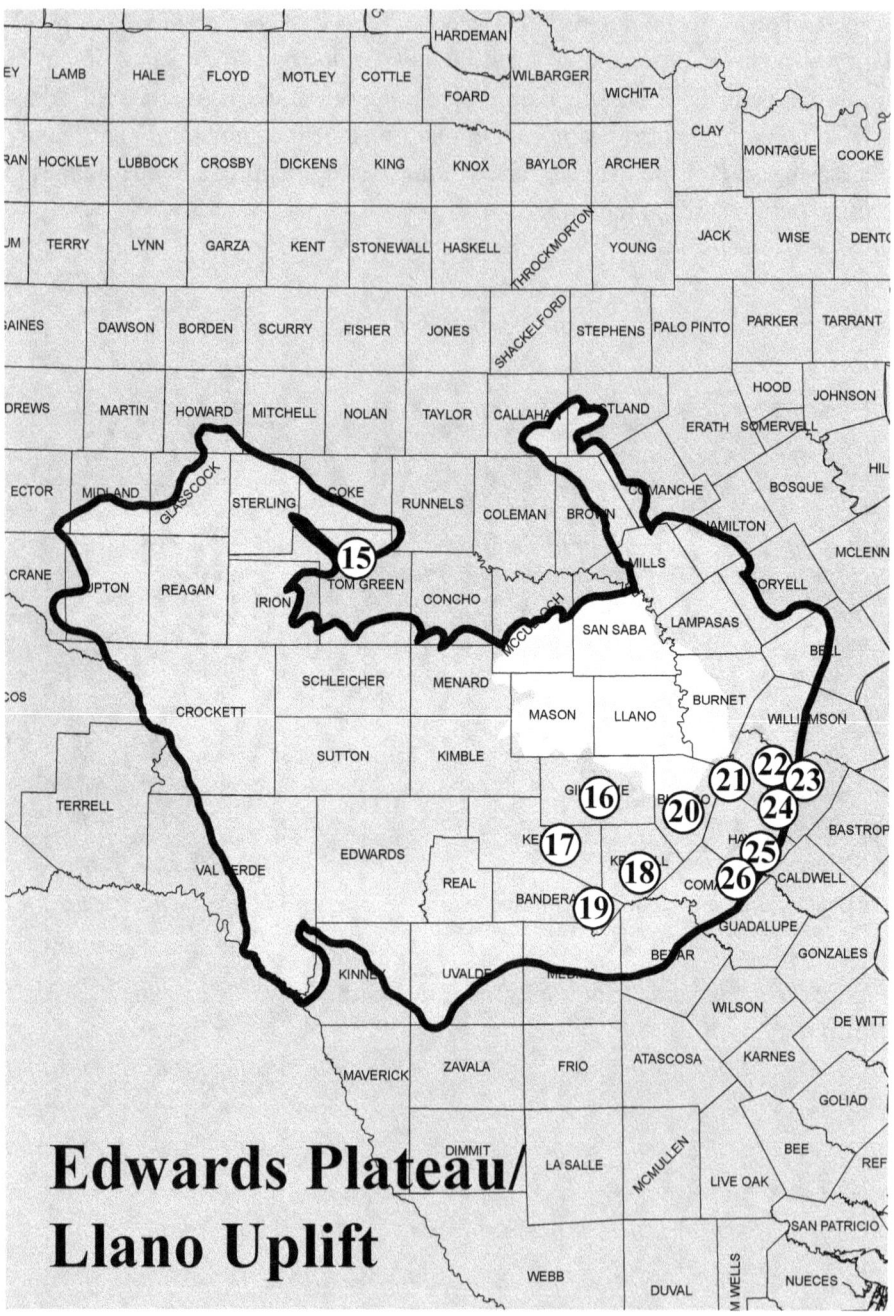

Figure 5—Facilities in the Edwards Plateau and Llano Uplift regions

San Angelo Nature Center

7409 Knickerbocker Rd., San Angelo, TX 76904

Owner: City of San Angelo   **Size:** 61 acres

Contacts: Phone 325-942-0121; E-mail michael.price@sanangelotexas.us

Website: http://www.sanangelotexas.us/index.asp?Type=B_
BASIC&SEC=%7B00031FE3-CDFA-4F45-A7FE-06E279DEB6DA%7D

Natural Regions: Edwards Plateau/Rolling Plains

Major Ecosystem(s): Concho River Valley; Lake Nasworthy

Overview: Located at Lake Nasworthy in Mary Lee Park, SANC is a regional museum and learning center with displays, hiking trails, a gift shop, and a diverse collection of live animals including bobcats, alligators, and rattlesnakes. The Adopt-an-Animal program contributes to supporting animals at the center. The Discovery Room includes a small reference library. The Xeriscape Garden features native trees, shrubs, and flowers. The nature trail at Spillway Rd. covers 60 acres along the Middle Concho River. Trail markers correspond to a guide available at the center.

Fun for Kids: Birthday parties that feature interaction with live animals, including live snake feeding, can be scheduled. Nature day camps are held for 2 weeks in June.

Family Fun: Nature Nights are sleepovers for kids and adults and include dinner, breakfast, and learning about nocturnal animals and other interactions with live animals.

The nature trail along the Middle Concho River has a self-guide brochure.

Educational: Interpretive tours can be scheduled by any type of group. The tours discuss many aspects of Concho Valley plants and animals and include one-on-one interaction with live animals and a live snake feeding.

Directions: From the intersection of Highways 67 and 87 in San Angelo, go south on S. Abe St./S. Bryant Blvd. (US 277/US 87). Go west on Knickerbocker Rd. about 6 miles to the center.

GPS Coordinates: Latitude: 31°22.587´ N   Longitude: 100°29.419´ W

The San Angelo Nature Center VC

Live animal exhibits, such as these tiger salamanders, in the VC

"Wild" prairie dogs behind the VC

Fredericksburg Nature Center

P.O. Box 2082, Fredericksburg, TX 78624

Owner: Friends of the FNC; City of Fredericksburg   **Size:** 10 acres

Contacts: Phone 830-997-4202; E-mail info@fredericksburgnaturecenter.org

Website: www.fredericksburgnaturecenter.org

Natural Region: Edwards Plateau

Major Ecosystem(s): Live Oak Creek and floodplain

Overview: FNC is located in Lady Bird Johnson Park about 3.5 miles southwest of downtown Fredericksburg on Hwy 16. The site consists of a small reservoir on Live Oak Creek, prairie remnants, some post oak savanna, and live oak-Ashe juniper woods. The creek and reservoir support several aquatic and wetland habitats.

Facilities include three interpretive nature trails including a 600-yard long wheelchair-accessible trail and bird watching blind. There is no interpretive center on site at this time, but several educational programs are offered off-site.

Fun for Kids: One mile of interpretive trails with a self-guide brochure. Online checklists for plants and animals can be printed. Guided trail walks by request only.

Family Fun: The Wings Over the Hills Nature Festival (http://www. WINGSTX.org) during the last weekend in April features birds, bats, butterflies, dragonflies, and wildflowers. The nature trails are located in Lady Bird Johnson Park.

Educational: The monthly Nature Series programs during the school year deal with many aspects of Hill Country ecology. These programs are held in the evening and are free to the public. FFNC volunteers also led trail walks, the annual third grade Day in the Park, and teacher training programs.

Directions: From downtown Fredericksburg, go about 3.5 miles south on Hwy 16. Turn right on Lady Bird Dr., then about 0.5 mile to parking area. The website includes a link to a map.

GPS Coordinates: Latitude: 30° 14.157′ N   Longitude: 98° 54.277′ W

The Fredericksburg Nature Center's nature trail in Lady Bird Johnson Park

A wheelchair-accessible bird-watching blind/feeding site

Riverside Nature Center

150 Francisco Lemos St., Kerrville, TX 78028

Owner: Riverside Nature Center Assoc.   **Size:** 5 acres

Contacts: Phone 830-257-4837; Fax 830-257-7844; E-mail office@riverside-naturecenter.org

Website: www.riversidenaturecenter.org

Natural Region: Edwards Plateau

Major Ecosystem(s): Guadalupe River watershed; live oak-mesquite-Ashe juniper parks

Overview: RNC is located at the confluence of Town Creek and the Guadalupe River, which rises from Edwards Aquifer springs in western Kerr County. The arboretum features native plants including 140 species of trees and 200 species of wildflowers. A trail along the Guadalupe features riparian habitat and wildlife. There is a sensory garden with Braille signs for the visually impaired.

The VC has displays that are rotated quarterly and usually include live animals. Gardens and trails are self-guided and are free to individuals. Group tours should be arranged in advance. The VC and some trails are wheelchair accessible. A free e-mail newsletter is available.

Fun for Kids: Special scouting programs for specific badges are offered. There is a Junior Naturalist program for grades 1–5. Summer nature day camps are for grades 3–6. The VC has a store/gift shop.

Family Fun: Special events about Hill Country habitat, conservation, plants, and animals occur throughout the year. One such event is Earth Day in April.

Educational: There are various nature education programs for grades K–8 that are aligned with state education standards. These are held in the spring and fall and are led by trained nature guides. Outreach programs for schools, homeschool programs, and community forums can be arranged. There is a lending library for members.

Directions: From I-10 north of Kerrville, go south on Hwy 16 (Fredericksburg Rd.) to downtown Kerrville. Turn west on Main St. (Hwy 27), then south on Francisco Lemos St. The website includes a printable map.

GPS Coordinates: Latitude: 30° 03.017´ N   Longitude: 99° 08.895´ W

The Riverside Nature Center VC

The Nature Study Lab at Riverside Nature Center

An Earth Day monarch butterfly parade at Riverside Nature Center

18 Cibolo Nature Center

140 City Park Rd., Boerne, TX 78006

Owner: City of Boerne/Friends of the Cibolo Wilderness   **Size:** 160 acres

Contacts: Phone 830-249-4616; E-mail nature@cibolo.org

Website: www.cibolo.org

Natural Region: Edwards Plateau

Major Ecosystem(s): Cibolo Creek watershed

Overview: CNC features examples of four different habitats: riparian forest along the creek, tall grass prairie, live oak savanna, and a restored spring-fed marsh. A 4-mile trail system includes a 0.25-mile boardwalk that crosses the marsh. The VC has hands-on displays for kids. The Lende Learning Center houses a wide variety of educational and recreational activities. A free e-mail newsletter is available.

The 60-acre Herff Farm at the Cibolo is an outdoor classroom for teaching the living skills nearly lost in little more than a generation, such as gardening, composting, beekeeping, and rainwater harvesting. The weekly farmers' market at the Herff Farm features Texas-produced organic or natural foods and products. An Inspiration Garden demonstrates organic gardening and water conservation, as well as container, raised bed, and square-foot gardening.

Fun for Kids: Summer day camps (nature adventure/art) are for kids ages 6–12.

Mother Nature's Storytime is for ages 3–5, and Kid's Club activities are for ages 3 and up. Scout badge programs are offered. The VC has a store.

Family Fun: The Songs & Stories outdoor concert series for families is held spring through fall. The Herff Farm weekly farmer's market is open in-season. The 4-mile trail system includes a boardwalk across the marsh and a dinosaur track display.

Educational: The Living in the Hill Country Series of classes and workshops for local landowners features land management, nature appreciation, and water issues. A Volunteer Citizen Scientist program offers land management research and service learning hours. The Outdoor Classroom program for school groups (K–8) emphasizes conservation of natural resources through a variety of activities and is aligned with state education standards. To arrange a school visit call or e-mail education@cibolo.org. Teacher training programs such as Project Wild, Aquatic Wild, Nature Box, and Monarch Monitoring are offered occasionally.

Directions: From San Antonio, take I-10 west about 30 miles to Boerne exit 542 (Hwy 87 North). Follow 87 to downtown Boerne. Turn right on Hwy 46E (River Rd.). Go about 1 mile, turn right onto City Park Rd., and go almost to the end. The website includes a printable map.

GPS Coordinates: Latitude: 29° 46.999ʹ N   Longitude: 98° 42.529ʹ W

The VC at the Cibolo Nature Center

The dinosaur trackway at the Cibolo Nature Center

The wetland boardwalk at the Cibolo Nature Center

Bear Springs Blossom Nature Preserve

P.O. Box 63295, Pipe Creek, TX 78063

Owner: BSB Nature Conservation Group, Inc.   **Size:** 125 acres

Contacts: Phone 830-460-0814; E-mail bearspringsblossom@yahoo.com

Website: www.bear-springs-blossom.org

Natural Region: Edwards Plateau

Major Ecosystem(s): Pipe Creek riparian corridor; live oak-Ashe juniper woods/parks

Overview: The property was formerly part of Bear Springs Ranch. Overgrazing and soil erosion resulted in typical Hill Country forests and parks dominated by live oak and Ashe juniper (cedar). Pipe Creek is an intermittent stream with narrow corridors of riparian trees and shrubs. The property has several hundred Texas madrone trees.

There are displays of local plants and animals and changing seasonal exhibits. There is a wildlife attraction area, fossil collection, and small library. Outdoor gardens featuring wildflowers and herbs attract birds and butterflies in season. Several pairs of endangered golden-cheeked warblers nest on the property.

Fun for Kids: There are 11 miles of nature/birding/hiking trails and a wildlife attraction area and seasonal butterfly/bird gardens. The main trail is wheelchair accessible. There are changing seasonal exhibits in the nature center.

Family Fun: Guided tours for individuals or groups are available year-round by appointment only. Seasonal nature walks include wildflower walks, fall foliage walks, and early morning bird walks. In summer, evening nature walks feature nocturnal wildlife.

Educational: School outreach programs on a wide variety of natural history and environmental topics are available. Special workshops and presentations include Hill Country geology, use of renewable energy, rainwater harvesting, building a home in the Hill Country, native plant advice, land stewardship, and other topics. Online nature and environmental education programs are offered.

Directions: Located about 10 miles east of Bandera on SH 16. Turn north onto Bear Springs Rd. at the Heart of Texas Wildlife Trail sign (HOTW 047), then left onto West Bear Springs Rd. Call for detailed directions from SH 16.

GPS Coordinates: Latitude: 29° 46.055´ N   Longitude: 98° 55.986´ W

The Bear Springs Blossom Nature Center & Preserve, with my dog Roxy in the foreground

A small wind turbine at Bear Springs Blossom

20 Selah Bamberger Ranch Preserve

2341 Blue Ridge Dr., Johnson City, TX 78636

Owner: Bamberger Ranch Preserve Foundation   **Size:** 5,500 acres

Contacts: Phone 830-868-2630; Fax 830-868-4639; E-mail selah@bambergerranch.org

Website: http://bambergerranch.org/

Natural Region: Edwards Plateau

Major Ecosystem(s): Miller Creek headwaters; live oak-Ashe juniper woods; restored native grasslands

Overview: Selah is a biblical term in the Book of Psalms intended as an invitation to pause and reflect on the message. Visitors to SBRP are invited to pause and reflect on their role in the natural world. This is one of the largest private land habitat restoration projects in Texas. Mr. Bamberger, over the last 40 years, through the management of habitat, grazing, and wildlife, has restored this worn-out ranch from an Ashe juniper (cedar)-dominated forest to a site dominated by native grasses—as it was before the arrival of Europeans. Old springs now flow again. Hardwoods such as Lacey oak, red oak, escarpment black cherry, and redbud are present again. Maples, bald cypress, and endangered Texas snowbell trees have been planted along the drainage that becomes Miller Creek.

Facilities include The Center, a large meeting space with kitchen available for groups. There are other accommodations that can be rented by small groups or families. There is a system of nature trails with interpretive signage. The Grass Trail features a restored mid-grass prairie site. The Chiroptorium is a man-made bat cave designed to support up to one million Mexican free-tailed bats. The ranch also supports the largest herd of critically endangered scimitar-horned oryx (an African antelope) in the world as part of an international Species Survival program.

SBRP is a working ranch and not open to drop-in visits or hiking. All group tours and visitations are by advance reservation only.

Fun for Kids: Camp Selah is a 5-day nature camp in June for kids ages 9–13. Space is limited to 20 kids and requires an application process. Some scholarships are available. The man-made bat cave allows seasonal bat flight viewings. Madrone Lake offers fishing and swimming.

Family Fun: Public ranch tours last 3.5 hours and are intended for individuals or groups of less than 20. Group tours are for 20 or more. Transportation is on an open-air trailer with a shade bonnet that can accommodate a wheelchair. Overnight field trips with lodging and meals can be scheduled. Special events include a variety of field days (birding, wildflowers, etc.) and workshops (grass, trees, water, etc.). Hes' Heritage Country Store provides a glimpse of the past. A small astronomical observatory permits stargazing.

Educational: SBRP is a teaching preserve providing customized education programs for school groups from all over central Texas. Hands-on lessons in the earth and life sciences are aligned with state education standards for all grades/age groups. Programs are supported by on-site Cretaceous-period dinosaur tracks, marine fossil beds, creeks and ponds for aquatic studies, nature trail system, man-made bat cave, livestock and ranching demonstrations, and heritage conservation at the Hes' Country Store. Day trips range from 3 to 8 hours. Overnight field trips with lodging and meals can be scheduled. Facilities include a small astronomical observatory. Grants may be available to cover field trip expenses for Title 1 schools. Science Camp for Teachers is a 3-day/2-night camp for third–fifth grade science teachers for CPE credits.

Directions: SBRP is in Blanco County south of Johnson City about 1 hour west of Austin and 1 hour north of San Antonio. All tours and visitations are by reservation. Directions are provided in advance of tours. Directions provided by GPS units tend to be inaccurate for this location.

The Center at Selah Bamberger Ranch Preserve

Hes' Heritage Store at Selah Bamberger Ranch

The man-made bat cave at Selah Bamberger Ranch

The small observatory at Selah Bamberger Ranch

²¹ Westcave Outdoor Discovery Center

24814 Hamilton Pool Rd., Round Mountain, TX 78663

Owner: Westcave Preserve Corp./Lower Colorado River Authority
Size: 75 acres

Contacts: Phone 830-825-3442; Fax 830-825-3509;
E-mail info@westcave.org

Website: http://westcave.org/

Natural Region: Edwards Plateau

Major Ecosystem(s): Pedernales River watershed (Heinz Branch Creek)

Overview: This facility is adjacent to the Pedernales River about 27 miles west of downtown Austin. The habitat is live oak-Ashe juniper savanna. Heinz Branch Creek flows through a limestone canyon lined by cypress trees and other riparian trees and shrubs. The centerpiece of the site is a 40-foot waterfall that flows over fern-covered travertine columns into a deep emerald pool.

The Warren Skaaren Environmental Learning Center features a number of sustainable building design concepts including a constructed wetland, geothermal heating/cooling, and rainwater collection. Entrance to the building is free. Visitation of the canyon, grotto, and cave is by guided tours only to minimize impacts to this fragile site. Public tours are scheduled year-round, weather permitting, 4 times daily. Tours are available to the first 30 visitors for each tour time; no reservations are taken.

Fun for Kids: The building features a solar observatory demonstrating the earth's changing position in relation to the sun.

Family Fun: Family Owl Prowls and other family programs are offered. Guided tours to the canyon, grotto, 40-foot waterfall, pool, and cave are available.

Educational: Student programs include guided tours of the preserve and exhibits at the Environmental Learning Center. Exhibits include geology, water, weather, and energy, and their connection to the plants and animals of the preserve. Weekday tours for schools and other organized groups must be scheduled ahead. Standard programs are aligned with state education standards and can be customized to meet the group's needs. Teacher resources correlated to state education standards are available. Teacher training programs like Project WILD are offered occasionally.

The Westcave Roundtable hosts landowners and other stakeholders interested in preserving the lower Pedernales River watershed.

Directions: From Austin, go west on Hwy 71 to the village of Bee Caves. Turn left at RR 3238 (Hamilton Pool Rd.). Go 14.5 miles to the Pedernales River. The preserve is the first gate on the right after crossing the river. The website includes a printable map.

GPS Coordinates: Latitude: 30° 20.166´ N   Longitude: 98° 08.485´ W

The Westcave Preserve Environmental Learning Center

The solar observatory at Westcave Preserve

22 Wild Basin Creative Research Center

805 N. Capital of Texas Highway, Austin, TX 78746

Owner: St. Edwards University; Travis County   **Size:** 227 acres

Contacts: Phone 512-327-7622; Fax 512-328-5632; E-mail mailto:wbasin@ stedwards.edu

Website: http://think.stedwards.edu/wildbasin/

Natural Region: Edwards Plateau

Major Ecosystem(s): Balcones canyon lands; Colorado River watershed

Overview: Located in the Hill Country just west of Austin, this facility has over 3 miles of hiking trails through live oak-Ashe juniper woods, grassland, and streamside (Bee Creek) habitats. Wild Basin is part of the Balcones Canyonlands Preserve that protects 8 endangered species and 27 species of concern.

The Easy Access Loop is stroller-friendly and assisted-handicap accessible. The area is open to the public from dawn until dusk daily. Pets, bicycles, and picnics are prohibited.

Fun for Kids: Over 3 miles of hiking trails include one that goes past a small waterfall on Bee Creek. There are bat houses and a chimney swift tower.

Family Fun: Special family events, such as the Austin Astronomical Society's evening stargazing programs, are offered. The Easy Access Loop trail is stroller friendly and accessible to the mobility impaired.

Educational: Guided 2-hour hikes for school groups give students (grades 1–5) hands-on outdoor experience and can be correlated to classroom studies in natural sciences. The preserve serves as an interdisciplinary environmental laboratory for St. Edwards University where students and faculty study ecological, behavioral, and biodiversity issues. Other schools and programs use Wild Basin as a case study for politics and local government and other disciplines.

The Trail Guide Training program prepares volunteers to lead guided hikes and tours.

Directions: The entrance is on the east side of Loop 360 (805 N. Capital of Texas Hwy), about 1 mile north of Bee Caves Rd., or about 3 miles south of Loop 360 bridge over Lake Austin (Colorado River). The website includes a printable map.

GPS Coordinates: Latitude: 30° 18.721' N   Longitude: 97° 49.577' W

The Wild Basin VC solar panels

The Wild Basin bat houses

The Wild Basin chimney swift tower

23 Austin Nature and Science Center

301 Nature Center Dr., Austin, TX 78746

Owner: City of Austin   **Size:** 20 acres

Contacts: Phone 512-974-3888; Fax 512-974-3885;
E-mail ANSC@austintexas.gov

Website: www.austintexas.gov/department/austin-nature-and-science-center

Natural Region: Edwards Plateau

Major Ecosystem(s): Lower Barton Creek/Barton Springs; live oak-Ashe juniper woods

Overview: ANSC is located on the extreme eastern edge of the Edwards Plateau over the Balcones Fault zone. As a component of Zilker Park, it has access to Lower Barton Creek and Barton Springs Pool where the Sheffield Education Center presents programs about the Edwards Aquifer and Barton Springs.

Public exhibits include native birds of prey, mammals, reptiles, invertebrates, a Naturalist Workshop, small ponds, an outdoor Dino Pit exhibit, and the 65-acre Zilker Nature Preserve with over 2 miles of hiking trails.

Personal visits are free; self-guided group tours have a modest fee and require reservations.

Fun for Kids: Nature's Way Preschool, for ages 3–5, meets September through May and encourages children to discover and explore the outdoors. The Naturalist Workshop has lot of stones, bones, fossils, animal skins, etc. The outdoor Dino Pit exhibit and play area lets young kids dig for fossils. Camps are offered during the summer and school breaks.

Family Fun: Hiking trails and lots of live native animals. A variety of public programs for families are offered throughout the year.

Educational: School programs are aligned with state education standards and are offered for pre-K–eighth grades. A teacher resource guide is available. After-school programs provide educational and recreational enhancement programs at school campuses and recreation centers. Additional programs include homeschool and Girl Scout programs.

Program topics include aquatic ecology, water conservation, fossils and geology, Edwards Aquifer/Barton Springs, animals, plants, adaptations, caving, and astronomy.

Directions: From MOPAC (Loop 1), take the 2244/Rollingwood exit and go east on Barton Springs Rd. Go left on Stratford Dr. Follow Stratford to the parking area under MOPAC bridge. Handicapped parking is available via a rear access road; call for directions. The website includes a map.

GPS Coordinates: Latitude: 30° 16.307˙N   Longitude: 97° 46.364˙W

The Austin Nature and Science Center VC

The Dino Pit activity area for kids

There are lots of live animals, such as this Harris hawk

Lady Bird Johnson Wildflower Center

4801 LaCrosse Ave., Austin, TX 78739

Owner: University of Texas-Austin   **Size:** 279 acres

Contacts: Phone 512-232-0100; Fax 512-232-0156; E-mail form on website

Website: www.wildflower.org

Natural Region: Edwards Plateau

Major Ecosystem(s): Live oak-Ashe juniper woods/parks; wildflower meadows

Overview: A native plant botanic garden and self-sustaining unit of UT-Austin, the Wildflower Center provides education programs for children and adults to teach people about their natural surroundings and how to grow native plants in their own backyards. The main gardens and meadows display over 600 kinds of native Texas wildflowers, trees, and shrubs, and include demonstrations of lawn options for homeowners and a butterfly garden. A research trail emphasizes central Texas ecology. Facilities model sustainability and include a rainwater collection system, large auditorium, art gallery with changing exhibits, store, café, library, research building, and growing operation.

The Little House features crafts and activities for kids. The McDermott Learning Center is a restored 19th century carriage house containing art exhibits. The grounds and buildings are wheelchair accessible except the observation tower and a couple of the trails.

This facility is across the street from the Veloway (www.veloway.com), a 3-mile paved loop exclusively for biking and rollerblading in Slaughter Creek Metropolitan Park.

Fun for Kids: The Texas Arboretum has swings, picnic tables, and over 50 species of Texas oaks. The Little House features nature crafts and activities. There is a butterfly garden.

Family Fun: Nature Nights are low-cost family programs exploring plants, animals, and central Texas ecology and feature interactive presentations, hikes with experts, and nature crafting for kids. Plant and seed sale festivals are held each spring and fall. There is a store, café, nature art gallery, and 5 picnic areas.

Educational: Go Native U is an informal adult education program about the sustainable use and conservation of native wildflowers, plants, and landscapes conducted at the center.

Self-guided group visits at discounted rates are available for pre-K through high school age youth. Available teacher resources include pre-trip/trip/post-trip activities. Docent-guided visits are available with advance notice. College classes can use the site as an outdoor classroom. The native plant online information network has a searchable database.

Directions: From Austin, go south on Loop 1 (MOPAC Expressway). Continue south past the light at Slaughter Ln. Turn left at the next light (LaCrosse Ave.) and proceed to LBJWC on the right near the end of LaCrosse. The website includes links to maps.

GPS Coordinates: Latitude: 30° 11.190´N   Longitude: 97° 52.272´W

The Lady Bird Johnson Wildflower Center

The Wildflower cafe and gardens at Lady Bird Johnson

25 Aquarena Center (Meadows Center for Water and the Environment)

921 Aquarena Springs Dr., San Marcos, TX 78666

Owner: Texas State University

Contacts: Phone 512-245-7570; E-mail rc13@txstate.edu

Website: www.aquarena.txstate.edu

Natural Region: Edwards Plateau

Major Ecosystem(s): San Marcos Springs/River

Overview: This facility is under the direction of the River Systems Institute at Texas State Univ. Here, Edwards Aquifer water emerges at San Marcos Springs to form Spring Lake—the headwaters of the San Marcos River. The center features extensive environmental education programs dealing with rivers, springs, and freshwater wetlands. About 200 springs form Spring Lake and provide habitats for 8 federally endangered or threatened species—3 salamanders, 2 fishes, 2 beetles, and an amphipod. A small aquarium exhibit in the Texas Rivers Center features the Texas blind salamander, San Marcos salamander, fountain darter, and American eel.

The site was formerly the Aquarena Springs water park. There are nature trails on the peninsula where all previous structures and asphalt from the theme park were removed and replaced with native grasslands. San Marcos Springs are the second largest in Texas. Comal Springs in New Braunfels are the largest in Texas and the southwestern U.S.

Fun for Kids: Summer day camps include elementary level camps and a junior high Stewardship Academy camp. Activities emphasize environmental themes. There are special programs for scout groups. The Texas Rivers Center has an aquarium with live fish and amphibians, and a baby turtle tank.

Family Fun: The floating wetlands boardwalk is a self-guided trail featuring the effects of invasive species on wetland habitats. Glass-bottom boat and glass-bottom kayak tours are offered. A Groundwater Festival is held every fall.

Educational: Interpreter-led field trips and private group tours can be customized to meet specific grade level and classroom learning goals. Tours can be teacher-led except for the glass-bottom boat segment. Tours for teachers present an overview of the educational programs and objectives. Classroom resources for teachers are available.

Diving for Science (scuba) authorization classes are conducted.

Directions: In San Marcos, take exit 206 off I-35. Stay on the access road. Merge right onto Aquarena Springs Dr./Loop 82. Go through 2 traffic lights and cross the railroad tracks. Take a right onto Laurel Ridge and continue through the golf course to the entrance. The website includes a printable map.

GPS Coordinates: Latitude: 29° 53.651´ N   Longitude: 97° 55.747´ W

The Aquarena Center Discovery Hall

The glass-bottomed boat tour at Aquarena Center

San Marcos Nature Center

430 Riverside Dr., San Marcos, TX 78666

Owner: City of San Marcos   **Size:** about 3 acres

Contacts: Phone 512-393-8447; E-mail jwinters@sanmarcostx.gov

Website: www.ci.san-marcos.tx.us/index.aspx?page=796

Natural Region: Edwards Plateau

Major Ecosystem(s): San Marcos River watershed (urban)

Overview: Located in Crook Park, SMNC is owned and operated by the City of San Marcos. It is also the San Marcos River birding trailhead. It has indoor live animal exhibits and an outdoor wildscape of native plants typical of the area. The wildscape features a pond, animal habitats, wildflower exhibits, multiple gardens of native plants with identifying markers, a butterfly house, a bird-watching blind, and in general serves as an outdoor learning center. The butterfly house provides food and habitat for at least 7 local species of butterflies and includes a separate nursery for cocoons.

There is no fee with the exception of a nominal charge for adults (over 12 years) visiting the butterfly house.

Fun for Kids: Indoor live animal exhibits include reptiles, amphibians, arachnids, and fish. There is a butterfly house and cocoon nursery. Summer and spring break day camps are available for kids ages 5–12. There are also some preschooler programs.

Family Fun: There are various seasonal events such as Halloween Creature Crawl, spring and fall San Marcos River cleanups, and the annual fall native plant sale and local artisan craft market. Tours of the facility and butterfly house are available daily pending staff availability. Various workshops and seminars are offered throughout the year and promote the use of native plants and wildlife education.

Educational: Environmental education programs for school and youth groups include environment and ecology, natural resources, plant growth and development, native wildlife, habitat conservation, gardening and outdoor recreation, and butterflies.

Directions: SMNC is in Crook Park at 430 Riverside Dr., next to the Tourist Information Center on the I-35 South access road.

GPS Coordinates: Latitude: 29° 52.626´N   Longitude: 97° 55.772´ W

The San Marcos Nature Center VC

Inside the butterfly house at the San Marcos Nature Center

A live giant tortoise at the San Marcos Nature Center

OAK WOODS & PRAIRIES/ BLACKLAND PRAIRIES

The two western fingers of the Oak Woods & Prairies region are also known as the Western and Eastern Cross Timbers because early settlers encountered belts of blackjack and post oak crossing the prairie grasslands. Sandwiched between the two fingers is a swath of Blackland Prairie known as the Grand Prairie.

During the Cretaceous period (144 to 66 million years ago), this area was on the edge of the continent and shallow seas advanced and retreated repeatedly over the area. Some of these ocean advances formed a north-south seaway that connected the Gulf of Mexico with the Arctic Ocean. In these Cretaceous seas, limestones were laid down in deeper waters and sandstones, shales, and other sedimentary rocks were laid down along shorelines and mudflats. Soils are typically sandy where the bedrock is sandstone, with strips and patches of dark-colored clays over shale bedrock. Blackjack and post oak prefer sandy soils and grasslands are found on clay soils.

The landscape in this part of these regions is rolling to hilly and elevations range from 500 to 800 feet. Average annual rainfall is 28 to 40 inches with a peak in late spring. The primary land use in this area is livestock grazing, mostly on "improved" pastures of Bermuda grass and other nonnative grasses. Of course, urban and suburban development has also consumed much of the area. Practically none of the native prairie grasslands can be found today. An exception is the Caddo/Lyndon B. Johnson National Grasslands, managed by the U.S. Forest Service, near Decatur in northeast Texas.

East and south of the old continental edge (the buried Ouachita Mountain range) are sand, gravel, and mud (clay) sediments from the eroding Rocky Mountains that were deposited by rivers into the Gulf of Mexico throughout the Tertiary period (66 to 2 million years ago). This deposition of sediment moved the coastline southward over 200 miles to the present Gulf coast. The sediment layers get progressively younger toward the Gulf and are 40 to 50 thousand feet deep on the coast!

The eastern part of the Oak Woods & Prairies region is also known as the Post Oak Savanna. It is a transition zone between the pine-hardwood forests to the east and the tallgrass prairie to the west. Near Bastrop are hilly exposures of the red Carrizo sandstone. These well-drained sandy ridges support pine trees. This area is known as the Lost Pines because the nearest other loblolly pine forests are far to the east in the Piney Woods region.

The landscape is gently rolling with elevations from 200 to 500 feet. Average annual rainfall varies from 30 to 45 inches. Floodplain forests along the drainages typically support elm, pecan, water oak, and hackberry. The major land uses are farming and livestock grazing. Most native grasslands are gone. Improved pastures are seeded to Bermuda grass and other introduced grasses. The region produces significant amounts of oil, gas, and lignite (a soft, dirty-burning brown coal).The fragmentation of natural habitats caused by smaller and smaller land holdings is rampant in the Post Oak Savanna north and west of Houston. This has caused many native plants and animals, like the endangered Houston toad, to decline or disappear from the region.

The Blackland Prairies are named for the dark, fertile, calcareous clay soils of the region. These "black gumbo" clay soils are dark because of the high organic matter content from the accumulation of dead grass over time. The native tallgrass prairies once found here supported grass species like big and little bluestem, Indiangrass, and switchgrass. Almost the entire region is now in crops or grazing land. Native prairie may be the most endangered of all Texas ecosystems. Those parcels that remain have been invaded by brush because of overgrazing and the suppression of natural wildfires.

Early German and Czech immigrants made cotton king in this region and cities on the edge of the region from Dallas/Fort Worth to San Antonio grew right along with agriculture.

The landscape is nearly flat to rolling and elevations range from 300 to 800 feet. Average annual rainfall varies from 28 inches in the west to 40 inches in the east. The floodplains of rivers crossing this region support the same trees as the Post Oak Savanna area but the riparian corridors are very narrow because the valuable croplands of the region are cleared right up to the stream banks.

Figure 6 shows the distribution of facilities in the Oaks Woods & Prairies and Blackland Prairies regions.

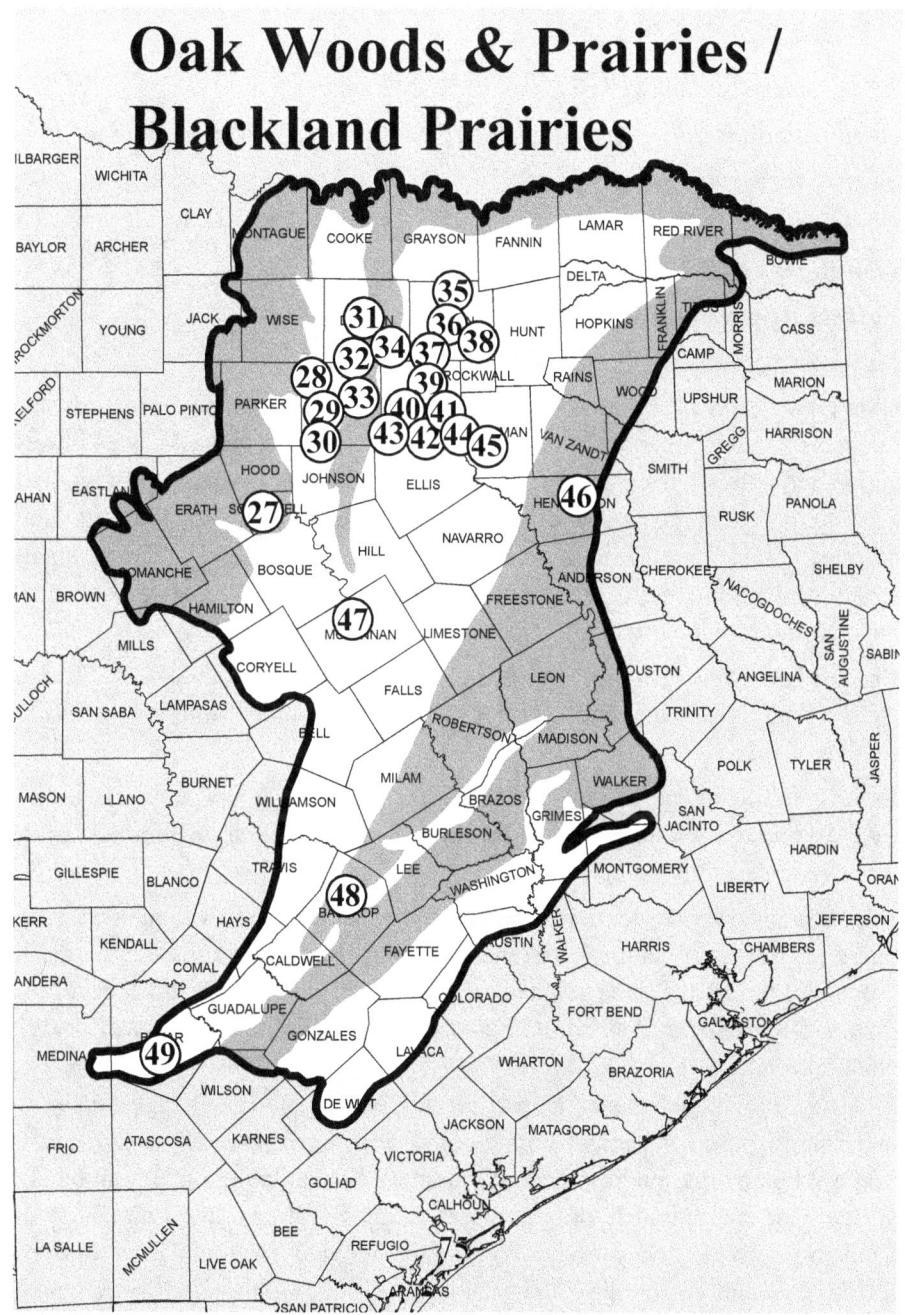

Figure 6—Facilities in the Oaks Woods & Prairies and Blackland Prairies regions

27 Fossil Rim Wildlife Center

2299 County Rd. 2008, Glen Rose, TX 76043

Owner: Earth Promise, doing business as Fossil Rim Wildlife Center

Size: 1,700 acres

Contacts: Phone 254-897-2960; E-mail form on website

Website: www.fossilrim.org

Natural Region: Oak Woods & Prairies

Major Ecosystem(s): Western Cross Timbers

Overview: FRWC specializes in breeding and management programs for threatened and endangered wildlife from Texas and around the world. Conservation and education are its main thrusts; but scientific research, professional training, and management and restoration of the natural habitats on its land are also emphasized. Guided or self-drive safari-like driving tours, a small lodgings operation, a gift store, a café, a children's animal center, and a membership program are the main attractions.

Fun for Kids: The Children's Animal Center features live animals. Wolf Ridge Nature Camp offers day and overnight camps year-round. Summer camps are for ages 7–17.

Family Fun: Guided or self-drive safari-like driving tours feature wildlife from around the world. Food can be purchased for feeding the animals. Limited on-site family lodging is available.

Educational: The education department offers a variety of guided tours, day and overnight camps, weekend programs and workshops, homeschool programs, field trips, etc., aligned with state education standards. Facilities include a butterfly garden, nature trails, and on-site lodging at the Wolf Ridge Nature Camp.

The Wolf Ridge Nature Camp offers day, overnight, scout badge, and summer camps. Summer camps for ages 7–17 are offered from June to August. Some scholarships for low-income kids may be available. Other camps are year-round. An outreach program for all ages features live animals with hands-on activities. Homeschool programs include class and tour options for all ages and customized homeschool events. A Homeschool Enrichment E-zine is available. Teacher workshops for CPE credit include Project WILD, Growing Up Wild, and Project Learning Tree.

Directions: From Glen Rose in Somervell County, about 60 miles southwest of Ft. Worth, go west on US 67 about 4 miles from Glen Rose. Turn left (south) onto CR 2008 and go about one 1.25 miles to the entrance. The website includes printable maps.

GPS Coordinates: Latitude: 32° 10.827'N   Longitude: 97° 47.794' W

The Fossil Rim Children's Animal Center

Bison at the Fossil Rim Wildlife Center

28 Fort Worth Nature Center & Refuge

9601 Fossil Ridge Rd., Fort Worth, TX 76135

Owner: City of Fort Worth   **Size:** 3,621 acres

Contacts: Phone 817-392-7410; Fax 817-392-7415; E-mail form on website

Website: www.fwnaturecenter.org

Natural Regions: Oak Woods & Prairies/Blackland Prairie

Major Ecosystem(s): Western Cross Timbers, Grand Prairie; West Fork of the Trinity River

Overview: FWNCR is one of the largest city-owned nature centers in the U.S. It is located in a transition zone between the Western Cross Timbers (post oak-tallgrass savanna) on the west and the Grand Prairie to the east. It straddles the West Fork of the Trinity.

Floodplain forests include trees like pecan, cottonwood, bur oak, and chinkapin oak. There are grasses and wildflowers typical of both tallgrass and mid-grass prairie, as well as post oak and live oak savannas. There is also a bison herd and a prairie dog town.

Almost 1,000 acres of wetlands features an 800-foot boardwalk into a marsh that occupies a former channel of the Trinity River. There are over 20 miles of hiking trails.

Fun for Kids: There is a prairie dog town and bison herd as well as other live animals. The Preschool Discovery Club is for ages 3–5.

Family Fun: Weekend classes and hikes for families and individuals cover an array of topics. The hiking trails include an 800-foot marsh boardwalk. Canoe and kayak tours are available.

Educational: Naturalist-guided tours for schools and other groups discuss local plant and animal adaptations. Programs feature native plants and pollinators, and local animals and their adaptations for life. The Hardwicke Interpretive Center conducts live-animal education programs and other programs both on- and off-site for schools and groups. The Distance Learning program offers a wide range of presentations aligned with state education standards that will bring nature to you through interactive videoconferences.

The Botanical Research Institute of Texas (BRIT) maintains on its website (www.brit.org) a digital herbarium of plants collected at FWNCR.

Directions: Located on the northwestern edge of Fort Worth. From Loop I-820, exit onto Hwy 199 (Jacksboro Hwy) and go west 4 miles. Exit at Confederate Park Rd. to the right and stay on the service road. At the stop sign, turn right into FWNCR. The website includes a link to a printable map.

GPS Coordinates: Latitude: 32° 49.706' N   Longitude: 97° 28.761' W

The Fort Worth Nature Center Interpretive Center

A wildlife viewing station inside the Interpretive Center

28 Botanical Research Institute of Texas

1700 University Dr., Fort Worth, TX 76107

Owner: BRIT, Inc.   **Size:** over 5 acres

Contacts: Phone 817-332-4441; Fax 817-332-4112; E-mail form on website

Website: www.brit.org

Natural Region: Blackland Prairie

Major Ecosystem(s): Urban

Overview: Located on the Grand Prairie, this area is former floodplain forest of the Clear Fork of the Trinity River. BRIT's sustainable facility is adjacent to the Fort Worth Botanic Garden and many programs are in partnership with FWBG. The building has earned the LEED® platinum certification from the U.S. Green Building Council. It features a living roof with species native to the Grand Prairie.

The herbarium houses over one million dried plant specimens. The large library serves researchers and teachers. An important function of BRIT is teaching children and adults about the importance of plants to ecological sustainability and the importance of stewardship of local ecosystems.

Fun for Kids: Camp BRIT is a summer day camp for grades K–8 that allows kids to work alongside scientists. The Burk Children's Library features Bella's Story Time for preschool children.

Family Fun: Community events, tours, public lectures, seminars, and educational exhibits are offered. Picnic sites are available across the street in Trinity Park. The building features native Texas prairie landscaping.

Educational: BRIT offers a variety of field trips and science programs in botany, ecology, and environmental science for K–12 public, private, and homeschool groups. All programs are aligned with state education standards. Programs emphasize local ecology, sustainability, and stewardship. Teacher training workshops for CPE credit include classroom and field training and focus on inquiry learning in the outdoors. The Teacher Resource Center includes curriculum guides, classroom kits and trunks, books, and videos. Adult education courses are offered.

Directions: From downtown Fort Worth, go west 1.5 miles on I-30. Exit at University Dr. and go north. BRIT is just north of the Fort Worth Botanic Garden at the southwest corner of University Dr. and Harley Ave. The website includes a printable map.

GPS Coordinates: Latitude: 32° 44.420ʹ N   Longitude: 97° 21.733ʹ W

The Botanical Research Institute of Texas (note the native prairie growing on the roof)

The Tree House room at BRIT

30 Fort Worth Botanic Garden

3220 Botanic Garden Blvd., Fort Worth, TX 76107

Owner: City of Fort Worth   **Size:** 110 acres

Contacts: Phone 817-392-5510; Fax 817-392-5539;
E-mail bgedu@fortworthtexas.gov

Website: http://fwbg.org/

Natural Region: Blackland Prairie

Major Ecosystem(s): Urban

Overview: Located on the Grand Prairie, this area is former floodplain forest of the Clear Fork of the Trinity River. FWBG is adjacent to the Botanical Research Institute of Texas and has many joint programs with BRIT. It is the oldest botanic garden in Texas. It features ponds, creeks, wooded areas, meadows, and 23 specialty gardens. The Tropical Conservatory houses a rainforest and self-guided or docent-guided tours are available. The Texas Native Forest Boardwalk is 995 feet long and features 13 interactive education stations dealing with forest ecology and featuring Texas native trees and shrubs.

Facilities include a VC, restaurant, and two gift shops. Picnic sites are available in Trinity Park across University Dr.

Fun for Kids: Summer day camps, holiday programs, and evening activities are offered for grades K–5 grades through the Green Thumb Club. Other features include the children's vegetable garden and the rainforest in the Tropical Conservatory.

Family Fun: The Texas Native Forest boardwalk features interactive education stations. Customized, downloadable Walk About-Talk About tours can be created online. There is a restaurant and two gift shops, and picnic sites are available across the street in Trinity Park. Spring and fall plant sales are held.

Educational: A variety of educational programs for children and adults are offered. All school programs are aligned with state education standards. For school groups, guided tours of select gardens or classroom learning combined with a garden exploration activity are available. There are programs for all grade levels. Self-guided or docent-guided tours are offered. Classes or families can create online a personalized Walk About-Talk About for a customized field trip.

For adults, your group can book a guided behind-the-scenes tour or schedule a speaker.

Directions: From downtown Fort Worth, go 1.5 miles west on I-30 and exit at University Dr. Go north on University Dr. FWBG has two entrances on your left. The Garden Center is at the second entrance. The website includes a printable map.

GPS Coordinates: Latitude: 32° 44.492˙N   Longitude: 97° 21.851˙W

The Fort Worth Botanic Garden and Conservatory

The Tropical Conservatory

The Texas Native Forest Boardwalk

³¹ Elm Fork Education Center

1704 W. Mulberry St., Denton, TX 76201

Owner: University of North Texas   **Size:** 117,000 sq. ft.

Contacts: Phone 940-565-4912; Fax 940-565-4297;
E-mail elmfork@unt.edu

Website: http://efec.unt.edu/

Natural Region: Blackland Prairie/Oak Woods & Prairies

Major Ecosystem(s): Urban

Overview: Historically, this area was transitional between the Grand Prairie and the Eastern Cross Timbers. EFEC is the public education branch of UNT's environmental programs and is located in the Environmental Education, Science, and Technology (EESAT) building on the Denton campus.

    The facility includes the large Eagle Exhibit Hall, the Sky Theatre planetarium, and the Outdoor Environmental Learning Area (ODELA). ODELA is a 7,000-sq.-ft. aquatic, geological, and archeological classroom for hands-on exploration by students of all ages.

Fun for Kids: Girl Scouts have opportunities for Try-Its and to earn badges. Summer Explorer's Camp offers age-appropriate scientific adventures for second–eighth graders.

Family Fun: Family fun science events on Saturdays allow parents and kids to interact and learn in a fair-like setting featuring a variety of science topics.

Educational: The Environmental Discovery Adventure program is a school field trip experience that features interactive activities in the exhibit hall, Sky Theater, and ODELA. Programs are grade specific for grades K–8 and aligned with state education standards. Teacher resources include online curricula for field trips with pre-visit, on-site, and post-visit materials. The Home School Labs Series offers courses in science and math for students of all ages.

Directions: From I-35E in Denton, exit 466B to North Texas Blvd. Continue to the second stop sign at West Hickory. Turn right on West Hickory, go 1.5 blocks (past Ave. D), and turn right into the EESAT parking lot. Get a visitor's pass inside. The website includes a printable map.

GPS Coordinates: Latitude: 33° 12.828ʹ N   Longitude: 97° 09.130ʹ W

The Environmental Education, Science, and Technology (FFSAT) building on the University of North Texas campus

The Elm Fork Education Center in the EESAT building

32 Bob Jones Nature Center & Preserve

355 E. Bob Jones Rd., Southlake, TX 76092

Owner: City of Southlake; Bob Jones NC, Inc. (operator)   **Size:** 76 acres

Contacts: Phone 817-491-6333; E-mail bobjonesnaturecenter@hotmail.com

Website: http://www.bjnc.org/

Natural Region: Oak Woods & Prairies

Major Ecosystem(s): Eastern Cross Timbers remnant prairie, post oak savanna

Overview: BJNCP includes a relatively rare remnant of original post oak savanna from the Eastern Cross Timbers ecosystem. There are also some fine examples of restored remnant prairie and a pond.

Facilities include the VC with gift shop and changing exhibits, an old barn, a butterfly garden, a picnic pavilion, and hiking trails. Access is available to the 400-acre Walnut Grove National Recreation Trail administered by the U.S. Army Corps of Engineers as part of Grapevine Lake's public facilities. There is no entrance fee to the preserve, which is a city of Southlake park.

Fun For Kids: Scouting programs are offered as well as service project opportunities. Summer camps for ages 3–10 emphasize natural and physical sciences. Young Explorers classes (ages 3–6) and Adventure Club (ages 5–9)

emphasize hands-on science. Tuesday Trekkers is preschool classes for ages 4 and 5. Toddler Thursdays are for ages 2 and 3.

Family Fun: The VC features changing exhibits on topics such as pollinators, natural history of the area, etc. Guided tours and programs are available after school or on Saturdays. There are hiking trails, a picnic pavilion, and access to the Walnut Grove National Recreation Trail adjacent to Grapevine Lake.

Educational: Guided school/group field trips and programs are available. Homeschool workshops with various themes are offered on designated Fridays. Some adult classes (nature photography, painting/mixed media, edible wild plants, bird walks, etc.) are offered. Teacher workshops (Project WILD, WILD Aquatic) for CPE credit are offered periodically.

Directions: From Hwy 114 between Grapevine and Westlake, take the N. White Chapel Blvd. exit and go north until you intersect E. Bob Jones Rd. Turn right and go 0.5 mile to the entrance on your right just before Walnut Ln. The website includes a printable map.

GPS Coordinates: Latitude: 32° 59.864´ N   Longitude: 97° 08.891´ W

The Bob Jones Nature Center VC

The old barn at the Bob Jones Nature Center

33 River Legacy Living Science Center

703 NW Green Oaks Blvd. (at Cooper St.), Arlington, TX 76006

Owner: City of Arlington; River Legacy Foundation   **Size:** 1,300 acres

Contacts: Phone 817-860-6752; Fax 817-860-1595; E-mail form on website

Website: http://www.riverlegacy.org/

Natural Regions: Blackland Prairie/Oak Woods & Prairies

Major Ecosystem(s): Eastern Cross Timbers; West Fork Trinity River floodplain

Overview: RLLSC is in an area transitional between the Grand Prairie and the Eastern Cross Timbers ecosystems. It is just out of the floodplain of the West Fork of the Trinity River. It is the gateway to 1,300 acres of River Legacy Parks with over 8 miles of paved hike and bike trails, as well as an off-road mountain bike trail. The building features a sustainable design and native plant landscaping. It also has a large interactive exhibit hall, self-exploration stations, classrooms, aquaria and terraria, riparian viewing room, outdoor observation decks, and a gift shop.

Fun for Kids: Summer classes are offered for pre-K–eighth grades. After-school clubs for K–sixth graders meet once a month after school. Nature

School, for ages 3–5, combines indoor and outdoor activities and meets September through May. Cub Scout badge programs are offered.

Family Fun: Public programs and festivals are offered on Saturdays for children and adults. Eight miles of paved hike/bike trails, an off-road mountain bike trail, and access to 1,300 acres of River Legacy Parks are available.

Educational: RLLSC partners with the Arlington ISD (including Title 1 schools) and the Eagle Mountain-Saginaw ISD. Field investigations are guided by naturalists for K–sixth grade groups. The Young Scientists program involves all Arlington ISD fourth graders and allows them to compare the ecology of RLLSC's woods to their own school yards. Homeschool programs are for ages 5–7 and 8–9. Self-guided tours can be scheduled. Professional development programs and teacher workshops help teachers bring nature into the classroom and qualify for CPE credit.

Directions: From I-30 in Arlington, take Exit 27 to N. Cooper St. Go north (left) on N. Cooper for about 1.5 miles to the entrance at the intersection with Green Oaks Blvd. The website includes links to printable maps.

GPS Coordinates: Latitude: 32° 47.002′ N   Longitude: 97° 06.902′ W

The River Legacy Living Science Center

A River Legacy outdoor nature class

34 Lewisville Lake Environmental Learning Area

201 E. Jones St., Lewisville, TX 75057

Owner: U.S. Army Corps of Engineers; LLELA Consortium (operator)   **Size:** 2,000 acres

Contacts: Phone 972-219-3930; E-mail mailto:lisacole@unt.edul

Website: http://www.ias.unt.edu/llela/main.htm

Natural Regions: Blackland Prairie/Oak Woods & Prairies

Major Ecosystem(s): Elm Fork of the Trinity River; Eastern Cross Timbers

Overview: LLELA sits below the Lewisville Lake dam. This area is transitional between the Eastern Cross Timbers and the Blackland Prairie. The lake is an impoundment on the Elm Fork of the Trinity River, which runs through the area. There are small remnants of tallgrass prairie, old growth Cross Timbers upland oak forest, and old growth bottomland forest. There are various types of permanent and temporary floodplain wetlands including sloughs, creeks, old stock ponds, Cottonwood Marsh, and the Beaver Pond Paddling Trail.

Research and restoration efforts are part of the LLELA mandate. The area also features a historic log homestead.

Fun for Kids: A variety of group camping opportunities, service projects, and badge workshops are offered to scout and other youth groups. Summer outdoor experiences (day camps) are offered for kids ages 7–12. These include a variety of ecological topics and outdoor activities.

Family Fun: LLELA is open to the general public Friday–Sunday for hiking, fishing, camping, paddling, birding, and the Minor-Porter log homestead tours. Family fun weekend tours and activities can include guided trail hikes and kayak tours.

Educational: School and group programs and tours can be scheduled any time. Field studies (Monday–Friday) include a variety of programs for all grade levels, including homeschools, and are aligned with state education standards. Programs include aquatic ecology, insects, birds, forests, and wildlife management. Customized programs can be scheduled. Guided trail hikes and kayak tours are offered, and themes for hikes can be supplied by the group leader or the LLELA guide. Self-guided hikes are also permitted. Teacher workshops such as Project WILD and Aquatic Project WILD for CPE credit are offered.

Directions: From I-35E in Lewisville, exit on Valley Ridge about 1 mile north of Business 121. Go east to the stoplight at Mill St. Turn north (left) on Mill St, and go to Jones St. Turn east (right) on Jones until it dead-ends at the gate at Jones and N. Kealy Ave. The website includes a printable map.

GPS Coordinates: Latitude: 33° 03.836´ N   Longitude: 96° 59.545´ W

The Lewisville Lake Environmental Learning Area entrance

The Minor-Porter log homestead at LLELA

35 Collin County Adventure Camp

1180 W. Houston St., Anna, TX 75409

Owner: Collin County; Greater Dallas YMCA   **Size:** 427 acres

Contacts: Phone 214-667-5600; Fax 972-924-8587; E-mail amassingill@ymcadallas.org

Website: www.ymcadallas.org/locations/collin_county_adventure_camp/

Natural Region: Blackland Prairie

Major Ecosystem(s): Prairie; creeks with riparian forest; ponds

Overview: CCAC is a joint venture of Collin County (landowner) and the Greater Dallas YMCA (operator). The camp can serve 500 campers. Facilities include a wide array of educational and recreational programs and equipment. There are 5 miles of trails, 8 teaching trail shelters, 3 lakes with piers, several creeks with bridges, prairie, forest, a wide variety of recreational fields and facilities, and a camp store. Cabins are air conditioned and heated.

During summer, the camp serves groups, families, and day campers. During the school year, community and school groups (mostly fifth graders from Collin County) are served during the week and other groups on weekends. Any age school group can be accommodated.

Fun for Kids: In addition to the ecology courses, a wide range of team building activities, such as challenge courses, are offered along with other outdoor activities like GPS hunts, paddling, climbing, archery, swimming, fishing, and team sports. Summer day camps are for ages 5–15.

Family Fun: The YMCA's Adventure Guide Program is designed for fathers and their young children. The camp serves families during the summer.

Educational: Fifth grade (and other groups) field trips—usually 3 days and 2 nights—emphasize forest, prairie, and aquatic ecology, and math in nature. All courses are aligned with state education standards. Day-only programs are also offered and students of all ages can be accommodated. Courses are taught by camp staff or by visiting teachers.

Directions: From Dallas, go north on US 75 (Central Expressway) and take exit 45 (Bonham exit, SH 121N) heading northeast. Stay right on 121N, following the sign to Trenton, for 10.3 miles. Go left on Hwy 2862 into Westminster for just over 1 mile to a 3-way stop at FM 3133. Go left (south) on FM 2862 and go 1 mile. The paved road turns right and is called W. Houston St. Go past the post office on the left and make the first right into the camp entrance. The website includes a printable map.

GPS Coordinates: Latitude: 33°21.888ʹN   Longitude: 96°28.408ʹW

The impressive Collin County Adventure Camp gate

The Adventure Camp education building

36 Heard Natural Science Museum & Wildlife Sanctuary

1 Nature Place, McKinney, TX 75069

Owner: HNSM&WS, Inc.   **Size:** 289 acres

Contacts: Phone 972-562-5566; Fax 972-548-9119; E-mail info@heardmuseum.org

Website: www.heardmuseum.org

Natural Region: Blackland Prairie

Major Ecosystem(s): Wilson Creek bottomland forest and wetlands; tallgrass prairie; upland forest

Overview: The Heard has 5 habitats: remnants of restored tallgrass prairie; bottomland hardwood forest along Wilson Creek; 60 acres of wetlands associated with the creek; upland forest; and limestone escarpment. Seven trails total 6.5 miles through these diverse habitats and include a boardwalk in the wetlands.

The main building houses collections and exhibits featuring Texas geology and ecosystems, live animals, shells from around the world, traveling exhibits, and a nature store with kid's corner. Other facilities include the outdoor Animals of the World exhibit, a 2-acre native plant garden, a seasonal butterfly house and garden, and the Science Resource Center and Outdoor Amphitheater. Picnic areas are available.

Fun for Kids: Summer nature camps for ages 5–14 include a variety of nature topics, art, and animal care. Scouting badge workshops and service projects are offered. There are live animal exhibits and a seasonal butterfly house and garden.

Family Fun: For families, scouts, and groups, the EcoAdventure paddling programs teach paddling and wetland ecology. The family-oriented Observation Station program (ages 16 and younger) encourages kids to self-educate about natural objects.

Educational: Field trips for school and homeschool groups include options such as live animal presentations, guided trails, and field investigations that combine hands-on experiments and classroom studies and are aligned with state standards. One- and 2-hour field investigations topics include aquatic habitat, birds, native plants, and environmental and earth science. An outreach program for pre-K–adult features live animals and mobile field investigations that can be customized. Teacher workshops such as Project WILD, WILD Aquatic, and Project Learning Tree are offered for CPE credit.

Directions: From Dallas, go north on US 75 (Central Expressway) and take Exit 37 (Stacey Rd.). Go east on Stacey about 1 mile. Turn left (north) onto Greenville/Hwy 5 and go about 2 miles to Country Club Rd./FM 1378. Turn right and go 1 mile to the entrance on the left. The website includes a link to a printable map.

GPS Coordinates: Latitude: 33° 09.444′ N   Longitude: 96° 36.917′ W

The Heard Museum VC

A botany class at the Heard

37 City of Plano Environmental Education Center

4116 West Plano Parkway, Plano, TX 75093

Owner: City of Plano   **Size:** less than 1 acre

Contacts: Phone 972-769-4130; Fax 972-769-4219; E-mail form on website

Website: www.plano.gov/index.aspx?NID=982

Natural Region: Blackland Prairie

Major Ecosystem(s): Urban creek and trees

Overview: Plano's only LEED® platinum certified green building serves the community as a model for energy efficiency and sustainable design. It is not a classic nature center. It features practices and materials that include renewable energy (solar and wind), rainwater harvesting, use of local and reused materials, energy-efficient appliances, sustainable building materials green roof, water conservation, and waste management practices. It also features a water efficient landscape and outdoor learning classroom with environmental discovery gardens.

Fun for Kids: The environmental discovery gardens include a natural creek. Scouting and afterschool programs are offered.

Family Fun: The outdoor Nature Explore Classroom has interpretive displays, interactive programs and a backyard compost demonstration site.

Educational: The purpose of the EEC is to educate and involve residents, community and environmental leaders, building professionals, and educators in environmental responsibility and to demonstrate sustainability concepts and practices. Education outreach includes interpretive displays and interactive programs, regional training workshops, and public presentations. Education includes school, afterschool, and scouting programs, field trips and tours, and scheduled speakers. There are classes and programs for all ages on recycling, composting, household chemicals, litter reduction, e-recycling, water and energy conservation, and air quality.

For a schedule of classes and programs, visit the https://livegreeninplano.obsres.com/ website.

Directions: In Plano, from the Dallas North Tollway or US 75 (Central Expressway), take West Plano Parkway to 4116.

GPS Coordinates: Latitude: 33° 00.799˙N   Longitude: 96° 46.396˙ W

The City of Plano Environmental Education Center

Outdoor activity stations at the City of Plano Environmental Education Center

Blackland Prairie Raptor Center

Brockdale Park at Lake Lavon, Lucas, TX 75002

Operator: BPRC   **Size:** 66 acres

Contacts: Phone 469-964-9696; E-mail info@bpraptorcenter.org

Website: www.bpraptorcenter.org

Natural Region: Blackland Prairie

Major Ecosystem(s): Tallgrass prairie; Lake Lavon

Overview: BPRC is a conservation education organization specializing in public education about the relationship between raptors such as hawks, falcons, and owls and healthy ecosystems. It is located in Brockdale Park on the shore of Lake Lavon near Lucas in Collin County. The land is leased from the U.S. Army Corps of Engineers.

Facilities include an outdoor classroom, native plant demonstration garden, and future plans for interpretive trails through restored prairie. A raptor hospital is also planned for the future. This facility is only open to the public during first Saturdays and other special events. The emphasis is on outreach programs featuring live hawks and owls.

Fun for Kids: There are live hawks and owls, hands-on discovery activities, and an annual fishing derby. A free quarterly e-newsletter is available.

Family Fun: Monthly on-site special programs (first Saturdays) feature hands-on discovery activities for all ages. Other special events include raptor photo days (get your picture taken with a live raptor) and the annual family fishing derby. The developed portion of Brockdale Park has restrooms and picnic sites.

Educational: The outreach program brings live birds to your school, home-school, youth group, or community organization. Presentations feature live birds and deal with the special adaptations and ecological importance of raptors. Programs are adaptable to ages 4 and up.

Directions: From Dallas, take US 75 (Central Expressway) to Allen. Exit at Bethany Rd. and go east about 6 miles. Bethany becomes Lucas Rd. (FM 3286). At the light, go east on FM 3286 about 0.5 mile. Turn onto Brockdale Park Rd. and go about 1.3 miles. BPRC is on the left.

GPS Coordinates: Latitude: 33°04.826′N   Longitude: 96°33.026′W

A raptor outreach class (photo courtesy of Erich Neupert of BPRC)

39 Dallas Arboretum & Botanical Gardens

8525 Garland Rd., Dallas, TX 75218

Owner: City of Dallas; Dallas Arboretum & Botanical Society (operator)

Size: 66 acres

Contacts: Phone 214-515-6500; E-mail info@dallasarboretum.org

Website: www.dallasarboretum.org

Natural Region: Blackland Prairie

Major Ecosystem(s): Urban gardens and forest; White Rock Lake

Overview: DABG features 66 acres of themed display and trial gardens on the shore of White Rock Lake just northeast of downtown Dallas. Other features include a visitor education facility with classrooms, Rosine Hall, the historic DeGolyer home, an orientation theatre, dining area, and gift shop. The Texas Pioneer Adventure and Texas Town includes kid-sized replicas of a sod house, teepee, and other buildings depicting life on the prairie. The Rory Myers Children's Adventure Garden (CAG) is 8 acres and features 150 interactive exhibits in 17 themed areas.

There are additional dining options, a concert area, picnic areas, a one-mile fitness trail, and a free tram for the mobility impaired.

Fun for Kids: Full- and half-day summer camps are for ages 4–12. Texas Pioneer Adventure and Texas Town feature kid-sized replica buildings, a teepee, and a covered wagon. The CAG offers hands-on exhibits on plants, animals, food, and energy for kids of all ages.

Family Fun: Throughout the year, seasonal festivals, concerts, and family activities are offered. There is a one-mile fitness trail and picnic areas. The CAG has exhibits for all ages including habitats and earth cycles, and the Exploration Center features the OmniGlobe that shows geographical, historical, and weather information for the continents and the world over time.

Educational: A variety of guided tours and educational programs aligned with state education standards are offered. Self-guided tours for pre-K–12 can be scheduled. Most of the guided field trips are for K–sixth grade. Scholarships and transportation funds are available for some programs including the CAG. Classroom lab programs (grades 1–6) deal with plants, soil, water, insects, photosynthesis, adaptations for life, and ecology. Classroom programs include outdoor hands-on components.

Outreach programs are aligned with state standards for pre-K–sixth grades and include after-school program opportunities. A variety of adult education classes dealing mostly with plants and gardening combine demonstrations, lectures, and hands-on activities.

Directions: From downtown Dallas, go east on I-30. Take Exit 48B onto the frontage road. Turn left onto E. Grand Ave. (TX 78). E. Grand becomes Garland Rd. Make a U-turn at Lakeland Dr. and the entrance is on the right. The website includes a printable map.

GPS Coordinates: Latitude: 32° 49.276´ N   Longitude: 96° 43.021´ W

The Dallas Arboretum & Botanical Gardens

The Texas Pioneer Adventure at the Dallas Arboretum

40 Perot Museum of Nature and Science

2201 N. Field St., Dallas, TX 75201

Owner: PMNS   **Size:** 180,000 sq. ft.

Contacts: Phone 214-428-5555; E-mail info@perotmuseum.org

Website: www.perotmuseum.org

Natural Region: Blackland Prairie

Major Ecosystem(s): Urban

Overview: PMNS features 11 permanent exhibition halls, a traveling exhibition hall, and an education wing with 6 learning labs. It also has a multimedia digital cinema, outdoor observation deck, a children's museum with an outdoor play space and courtyard, a café, and a store. The building incorporates many green and sustainable features such as a roof emphasizing Texas native plants, rainwater collection system, solar heated water, LED lighting, and recycled and locally sourced building materials.

Fun for Kids: There are scouting adventure programs and badge workshops, sleepovers at the museum, and day camps. These include full-day Discovery Camp for grades K–6 over spring break and in summer, half-day Discovery Camp Jr. for ages 3–4, and Little Explorers for ages 6 months–4 years with adult companion. There is a children's museum with outdoor play space and courtyard.

Family Fun: Discovery Days family festivals on designated weekends explore a variety of science topics with hands-on activities, live demos, and interactive exhibits.

Educational: A wide variety of in-house and outreach classroom programs for pre-K–12 are offered in the sciences, including natural/life/earth sciences. Programs are aligned with state education standards and designed to supplement curriculum with hands-on, inquiry-based labs. After-school programs are also available. ScienceCast is a videoconference hands-on distance learning program for schools. Teachers have online access to resources such as classroom program menus, exhibit and film guides, an annual teacher's guide, and also some professional development programs that qualify for CPE credit. Homeschool Days are offered at various times throughout the year.

Directions: PMNS is at the NW corner of Woodall Rodgers Freeway (Hwy 366) and N. Field St. in Victory Park near downtown Dallas. The website includes a link to a printable map.

GPS Coordinates: Latitude: 32° 47.137′ N   Longitude: 96° 48.406′ W

The Perot Museum of Nature & Science

Texas Discovery Gardens at Fair Park

3601 Martin Luther King, Jr. Blvd., Dallas, TX 75210

Owner: TDG; City of Dallas Park and Rec. Dept.   **Size:** 7.5 acres

Contacts: Phone 214-428-7476; Fax 214-428-5338;
E-mail TDG@TexasDiscoveryGardens.org

Website: http://texasdiscoverygardens.org/

Natural Region: Blackland Prairie

Major Ecosystem(s): Urban gardens; constructed pond; tropical butterfly conservatory

Overview: TDG is in Fair Park near the Children's Aquarium and is the first public garden in Texas to be certified 100 percent organic by the Texas Organic Research Center. The gardens feature native plants and nonnative plants that are adapted to North Texas and that provide habitat for native wildlife. The 13 themed areas include a butterfly habitat garden, native wildlife pond, and a scent garden. There is a Texas native plant collection and a tropical butterfly house and insectarium.

Other facilities include a gift shop, art gallery, and a picnic area.

Fun for Kids: Scouting programs include badge programs and community service opportunities for older scouts. Summer day camps for ages 3–13 emphasize the ecology and animals of the gardens.

Family Fun: There is a tropical butterfly house and insectarium and an annual butterfly plant sale.

Educational: TDG offers a variety of field trips called EarthKeepers® programs for pre-K–eighth grades. They also offer seminars with entomologists and/or horticulturists for high school students. These programs are aligned with state education standards. Topics include gardening, butterflies and other insects, math in nature, how terrariums work, composting, etc. These programs can include the butterfly house. Programs include a curriculum integration packet and pre- and post-visit activities.

The outreach program can bring science labs to the school and afterschool programs. Program content can be modified to meet curriculum or age needs. Teachers can earn CPE credits at weekend workshops and planned events. Various classes and workshops dealing mostly with organic gardening and gardening for butterflies are available to the general public.

Directions: From downtown Dallas, take I-30 east. Take Exit 47 (Second Ave./Fair Park). Turn left at the second light onto MLK, Jr. Blvd. and enter Fair Park at Gate Six. The website includes a printable map.

GPS Coordinates: Latitude: 32° 46.524' N   Longitude: 96° 45.669' W

The Texas Discovery Gardens at Fair Park

Inside the butterfly house at Texas Discovery Gardens

42 Trinity River Audubon Center

6500 Great Trinity Forest Way (formerly South Loop 12), Dallas, TX 75217

Owner: City of Dallas; National Audubon Society (operator)   **Size:** 120 acres

Contacts: Phone 214-398-8722; E-mail form on website

Website: http://trinityriver.audubon.org/

Natural Region: Blackland Prairie

Major Ecosystem(s): Trinity River floodplain wetlands, bottomland hardwood forest, grasslands

Overview: TRAC is about 8 minutes south of downtown Dallas in the 6,000-acre Great Trinity Forest, the largest urban bottomland hardwood forest in the U.S. In addition to the river and floodplain forest, there are floodplain wetlands and some grasslands and restored prairie. Facilities include hands-on exhibits, 5 miles of nature trails, a Children's Discovery Garden, and a nature store. The building incorporates sustainable features that earned it LEED® gold certification.

TRAC is the flagship for Audubon's education and conservation initiatives in Texas. The focus is on serving schoolchildren and providing nature-based learning experiences.

Fun for Kids: Different summer camps for grades K–5 and nature clubs for ages 5–12 are offered. There is a Children's Discovery Garden.

Family Fun: Discover Together family programs and workshops are offered. The Third Thursday program offers free entry the third Thursday of every month.

The Discover Citizen Science program allows the public to participate in scientific studies through Great Backyard Bird Count, Christmas Bird Count, Amphibian Watch, and Mussel Watch programs. An e-Bird Trail Tracker kiosk is available to log local bird sightings into Cornell Lab of Ornithology's birding database.

Educational: Guided Eco-Investigations are aligned with state education standards for grades pre-K–12 and include a 4-hour field trip with pond study and exhibit hall exploration. Teachers also get pre- and post-activity resources for the classroom. Self-guided field trips are also available. Audubon Conservation Workshops for grades 3–6 focus on unique Dallas ecosystems. Soundscape Science for grades 4–5 uses listening skills and sound recordings to strengthen science understanding and critical thinking skills.

Teacher workshops such as Project WILD, Growing Up Wild, and Schoolyard Ecology offer CPE credit and provide classroom resources to teachers.

Directions: From downtown Dallas, take I-45 south. Exit Loop 12 East (Great Trinity Forest Way) and go about 3 miles. The entrance is on the right. The website includes a printable map.

GPS Coordinates: Latitude: 32° 42.282ʹ N   Longitude: 96° 42.368ʹ W

The Trinity River Audubon Center VC

A large bird-watching blind at TRAC

43 Dogwood Canyon Audubon Center at Cedar Hill

1206 W. FM 1382, Cedar Hill, TX 75104

Owner: National Audubon Society   **Size:** 205 acres

Contacts: Phone 469-526-1980; Fax 972-291-6430; E-mail form on website

Website: http://dogwoodcanyon.audubon.org/

Natural Regions: Blackland Prairie/Oak Woods & Prairies

Major Ecosystem(s): Post oak woods/forest/grassland mosaic

Overview: DCAC is 16 miles south of downtown Dallas in Cedar Hill and is in a region that enjoys a convergence of species from other natural regions including flowering dogwood more typical of East Texas. The White Rock Escarpment is an uplifted area where white limestone of the Austin Chalk formation is exposed on the ridge crests. The forest here is dominated by oaks and Ashe juniper (cedar). There are over 1.5 miles of trails plus a 0.5-mile ADA-accessible trail on the canyon floor.

The 6,000-sq.-ft. education center includes a nature store and nature viewing room that are ADA-accessible by chair lift. The building incorporates sustainable features that earned it LEED® gold certification.

Fun for Kids: The Nature Play Area connects children with the natural world and features picnic areas, an arts and crafts grove, and a Toddler Trail for the smallest naturalists.

Family Fun: This facility is adjacent to Cedar Hill State Park on Joe Pool

Lake. The Discover Together program is a 2-hour workshop (various topics) for families with children ages 5–13. Family Fun Day festivals that deal with various ecological topics are offered occasionally. The First Thursday program offers free entry the first Thursday of every month. The nature store, nature viewing room, and a half-mile of trail are all ADA-accessible. Private guided tours are available.

Citizen science projects include eBird at Dogwood Canyon, Project FeederWatch, Christmas Bird Count, Invaders of Texas (a program to map and eliminate invasive plants at the canyon), and other projects.

Educational: Academic programs are offered to grades pre-K–12 and are aligned with state education standards. Eco-Investigation programs focus on the local ecology and habitats of the escarpment ecosystem, scientific observation, and stewardship of natural resources. Conservation workshops for grades 3–6 are 4-hour, staff-led field experiences that focus on the unique ecosystem of southwest Dallas County and engage students in conservation action.

Bird University for adults is a calendar of bird-related workshops, field trips, and citizen science activities held in a variety of North Texas locations. Interpretive and school program volunteer training is offered.

Directions: From Dallas, take I-35 south to Hwy 67 south. Go a few miles south of the I-20 intersection and take the FM 1382 exit. Turn right on 1382 and go west to the entrance of Cedar Hill State Park. Make a U-turn and go back to DCAC. The website includes a map.

GPS Coordinates: Latitude: 32° 36.844˙N   Longitude: 96° 58.224˙W

The Dogwood Canyon Audubon Center VC

44 Dallas ISD Environmental Education Center

1600 Bowers Rd., Seagoville, TX 75155

Owner: Dallas ISD   **Size:** 500 acres

Contacts: Phone 972-749-6900; Fax 972-749-6901

Website: http://www.dallasisd.org/Page/863

Natural Region: Blackland Prairie

Major Ecosystem(s): Post oak woods/savanna; grasslands/meadows (old field); ponds/creeks

Overview: The EEC is adjacent to the heavily wooded Dallas County Post Oak Preserve, which has a 12-acre lake used for some programs. Facilities include a 26,000-sq.-ft. museum building with orientation theatre, exhibits that emphasize ecosystems found on-site, fossil exhibits, leaf/insect/bird collections, and preserved animal specimens. Features include an 8-foot globe with interactive video stations, a dining hall and decks, four environmental learning labs, and the Nature Nook store.

There are 3 nature trails, a barn and petting farm, an outdoor classroom/ camping area, and a ropes course. The Live Animals Lab houses animals used in educational programs. Facilities include native plant gardens, two vegetable gardens, orchards and other plantings, and a greenhouse.

Fun for Kids: There is an eight-foot globe with interactive video stations. There is a barn and petting farm as well as a Live Animals Lab.

Family Fun: The EEC is open to the general public Monday–Friday and on certain special-event Saturdays. Guided trail walks and staff-taught programs are available as well as a covered pavilion with restrooms and grill. The area is adjacent to the Dallas County Post Oak Preserve, which has a 12-acre lake. There are 3 nature trails.

Educational: Staff-guided programs are available for all grades (pre-K–12) and feature local ecosystems, water and water chemistry, soil, rocks and minerals, local animals and plants, fossils, American Indians, animal adaptations, and endangered species and biodiversity. All programs are aligned with state education standards (bilingual instruction). Some programs are available to non-DISD groups for a nominal fee. DISD teachers who have attended training workshops can present self-guided programs.

Directions: From Dallas, go east on US 175 (toward Kaufman) to the Seagoville Rd./Kaufman St. exit in Seagoville. After exiting, go to the second stop sign at Environmental Way. Turn right on Environmental Way and go just over

1 mile. EEC is on the right through the gate and stone columns.

GPS Coordinates: Latitude: 32°38.529'N   Longitude: 96°34.214'W

The Dallas ISD Environmental Education Center

The DISD giant interactive globe exhibit

45 John Bunker Sands Wetland Center

655 Martin Ln., Seagoville, TX 75159

Owner: Rosewood Corp./North Texas Municipal Water District   **Size:** 1,840 acres

Contacts: Phone 972-474-9100; E-mail contact@wetlandcenter.com

Website: www.wetlandcenter.com/

Natural Region: Blackland Prairie

Major Ecosystem(s): East Fork of the Trinity River; constructed emergent wetlands

Overview: The floodplain forest here is dominated by water oak, elm, and hackberry. JBSWC is the educational component of the East Fork Wetland Project of the NTMWD. Water is taken from the East Fork of the Trinity River, the quality is improved (polished) as the water moves through the wetlands, and then pumped through a 43-mile pipeline to Lake Lavon. The project is one of the largest constructed wetlands in the U.S.

The building is 5,400 sq. ft. with an exhibit hall, research lab, classroom, observation deck, and over 0.5 mile of boardwalks in the wetlands with pavilions and an observation tower. The wetlands support many species of aquatic plants and birds.

Fun for Kids: There is a live alligator exhibit in the building. There are boardwalks and an observation tower in the wetlands.

Family Fun: JBSWC is open to the public without appointment on the first and third Saturdays each month and tours can be arranged during the week Tuesday through Friday. Occasional special events like the Mud Bug Festival are held.

Educational: Education programs for school districts in the NTMWD focus on wetland and river ecosystems, bird migration and adaptations, and water quality and conservation. There are full-day and half-day programs aligned with state education standards for all grade levels. Field investigation and hands-on science programs are designed for high school and middle school students. Homeschool classes are held on the second Wednesday of the month; all age ranges are accommodated. Occasional professional development workshops for teachers are held.

Directions: Located about 25 miles from downtown Dallas. From Dallas, take I-635 or I-20 to US 175 south toward Seagoville. Go past the Seagoville exits and exit onto FM 1389 south. Go about 2 miles to Martin Ln. Turn left onto

Martin Ln. and go to JBSWC on the right. The website includes a printable map.

GPS Coordinates: Latitude: 32°36.837'N   Longitude: 96°30.057'W

The John Bunker Sands Wetland Center

A live alligator exhibit at John Bunker Sands

John Bunker Sands constructed water treatment wetlands

46 Texas Freshwater Fisheries Center

5550 FM 2495, Athens, TX 75752

Owner: Texas Parks & Wildlife Dept.   **Size:** 106 acres

Contacts: Phone 903-676-2277; Fax 903-677-2694;
E-mail tffc@tpwd.texas.gov

Website: http://www.tpwd.state.tx.us/spdest/visitorcenters/tffc/

Natural Region: Oak Woods & Prairies

Major Ecosystem(s): Post oak woods/forest/grassland mosaic; constructed ponds/wetlands

Overview: Located 4 miles east of Athens and 75 miles southeast of Dallas, TFFC combines a VC, educational programs, and a production freshwater hatchery. The facility includes over 300,000 gallons of indoor and outdoor aquaria displaying native fish, waterfowl, alligators, and amphibians in recreated habitats. There is an ADA-compliant 1-mile self-guided wetlands trail with a pitcher plant bog, forest stream, and pond.

Other features include a live, interactive dive show, a gift shop with snacks, and both covered and open picnic areas. The 1-acre public fishing pond is very popular. A narrated tram tour takes visitors through the outdoor hatchery ponds.

Fun for Kids: Kids can fish in the public fishing lake. The interactive, live scuba diving show is very popular. Hunter education classes are offered at various times during the year.

Family Fun: Special community events such as Halloween at the Hatchery, Fireworks at the Fishery, and the Family Bluegill Fishing Tournament are scheduled throughout the year. Fly fishing instruction is available by reservation. TFFC has the Freshwater Fishing Hall of Fame, and is the home of the ShareLunker selective breeding program for trophy bass.

Educational: School and youth groups account for about one-third of the 60 thousand annual visitors. The education center focuses on aquatic wildlife in the state's freshwater streams, ponds, and lakes. Aquatic education for weekday school/club/scout groups (reservations required) includes activities such as a wetlands tour, fishing, study of aquatic invertebrates, water quality investigation, fish identification, the dive show, tram tour of the hatchery, and tour of the VC exhibits. Independent learning stations are available for self-guided study of water properties and aquatic organisms.

Special programs such as teacher workshops on aquatic education and other professional development classes and workshops are offered occasionally.

Directions: From Dallas, take US 175 south to Athens. Follow Loop 7 east to FM 2495. Turn left on FM 2495 and go about 3 miles to TFFC. The website includes a printable map.

GPS Coordinates: Latitude: 32° 13.264´N   Longitude: 95° 46.066´W

The live dive show at the Texas Freshwater Fisheries Center

Live alligators at TFFC

The kid's fishing pond at TFFC

Lake Waco Wetlands Research and Education Center

1752 Eichelberger Crossing Rd., Waco, TX 76702

Owner: City of Waco Water Utility Services   **Size:** 180 acres

Contacts: Phone 254-848-9654; Fax 254-848-9217;
E-mail noras@ci.waco.tx.us

Website: www.lakewacowetlands.com/home.html

Natural Region: Blackland Prairie

Major Ecosystem(s): North Bosque River floodplain; constructed wetlands

Overview: The 180-acre functioning wetland was created to mitigate habitat loss caused by raising the water level of Lake Waco by 7 feet. Nearly 11 million gallons of North Bosque River water are pumped through the wetlands daily. The 6,000-sq.-ft. Research and Education Center has an ADA-accessible indoor classroom and lab and informational and interactive displays. An ADA-accessible walking trail overlooks the wetlands. The area includes floodplain forest and a small patch of upland forest.

The wetlands are open to the public even when the Research and Education Center is closed.

Fun for Kids: There are interactive displays in the Research and Education Center.

Family Fun: The walking trail overlooking the wetlands is ADA-accessible. The area offers excellent bird-watching with over 185 species identified. Guided tours are available upon request.

Educational: LWW is a cooperative community environmental education project that provides educational opportunities for students and visitors of all ages. The facility augments existing and future water-related programs at Baylor University, provides professional technical training and support services, and implements outreach efforts to educate the community and local schoolchildren about reservoir systems and related water issues.

Programs for grades pre-K–12 include tours, hikes, and classroom programs and projects. Older students have specialized programs that incorporate LWW habitats. Programs include curricula for Project Aquatic WILD, Wonders of Wetlands, and Project WET. Core biology concepts are aligned with state education standards. Customized programs can be arranged.

Directions: From I-35, take Exit 330B onto SH 6 west. Go about 10 miles to the intersection of SH 6 and FM 185, turn right on FM 185, and go about 1

mile. Then turn left onto Eichelberger Crossing Rd. LWW is about 1.5 miles on the right. The website includes a printable map.

GPS Coordinates: Latitude: 31°36.493˙N   Longitude: 97°18.376˙W

The Lake Waco Wetlands Research and Education Center

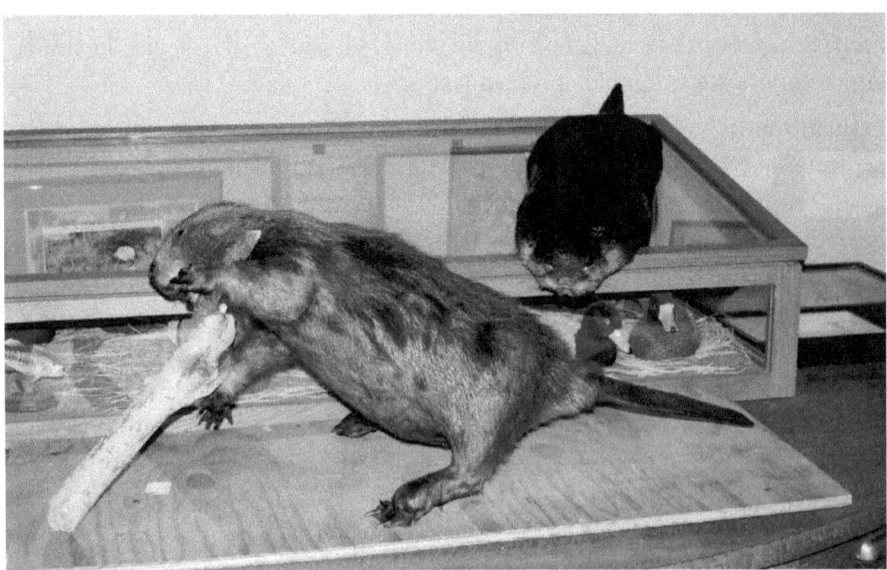

Lake Waco Wetlands wildlife exhibits

McKinney Roughs Nature Park

1884 Hwy 71 West, Cedar Creek, TX 78612

Owner: Lower Colorado River Authority   **Size:** 1,100 acres

Contacts: Phone 512-303-5073; Fax 512-303-5277;
E-mail outdoorprograms@lcra.org

Website: www.lcra.org/parks/developed_parks/mckinney_roughs.html

Natural Regions: Blackland Prairie/Oak Woods & Prairies

Major Ecosystem(s): Colorado River/riparian zone; post oak woods; prairie remnants; pine forest

Overview: MRNP is in a transition zone between the Blackland Prairie and Oak Woods & Prairies natural regions. It has 2 miles of frontage along the Colorado River with riparian forest. The Lost Pines ecosystem is about 10 miles to the east near Bastrop. McKinney Roughs has about 40 acres of loblolly pine forest believed to be the westernmost extension of the Lost Pines ecosystem.

The area is a day-use park with 18 miles of trails. The Natural Science Center features classrooms and labs. The VC has interactive exhibits and a gift shop.

Fun for Kids: Summer nature day camps for ages 6–15 offers an Austin-area shuttle service. River raft, canoe, and kayak trips can be scheduled. There is a team-building challenge course with low and high elements, including a zip-line.

Family Fun: Monthly family programs such as nature hikes and stargazing are free. Clubs or groups of more than 5 people should schedule a private hike. The area serves as a day-use park with 18 miles of trails.

Educational: A variety of community programs featuring natural science are offered. These include monthly river, recreation, and education programs. The Natural Science Center features science-based programs led by trained educators and professional staff. Teachers, homeschoolers, youth, and corporate groups can schedule day or overnight education programs dealing with water conservation, land stewardship, wildlife conservation, renewable energy, nighttime programs, orienteering and GPS use, river raft trips, and team-building challenge course activities. Academy in the Roughs offers 1- and 2-night programs with catered meals. River Days is an educational program, aligned with state education standards, that uses hands-on opportunities to teach stewardship and conservation of the Colorado River Basin.

Directions: From Austin, go 13 miles east of Austin Bergstrom International Airport on Hwy 71 West. The entrance to the park is on your left. The website includes an interactive map.

GPS Coordinates: Latitude: 30° 08.181´N   Longitude: 97° 27.580´W

The McKinney Roughs VC

The McKinney Roughs Natural Science Center

Mitchell Lake Audubon Center

10750 Pleasanton Rd., San Antonio, TX 78221

Owner: San Antonio Water System; National Audubon Society   **Size:** 1,200 acres

Contacts: Phone 210-628-1639; Fax 210-628-1642; E-mail form on website

Website: http://mitchelllake.audubon.org/

Natural Regions: Blackland Prairie/South Texas Brush Country

Major Ecosystem(s): Reservoir impoundments; mesquite-live oak-bluewood parks

Overview: MLAC is located just minutes from downtown San Antonio in the extreme southern tip of the Blackland Prairie region and on the extreme northern edge of the South Texas Brush Country region. The lake is 600 acres with 215 acres of wetlands and ponds and 385 acres of upland habitats. The building is a restored 1910 home with a xeriscape garden. The trees and shrubs of the area are typical of the South Texas Brush Country.

Audubon has partnered with the San Antonio Water System to connect schoolchildren and families to water-related science and issues in the San Antonio region. MLAC is open weekends and by appointment during the week.

Fun for Kids: There is a free Kids Birding program.

Family Fun: Public programs include birding tours, native plant walks and courses, docent training and volunteer days, and free family programs such as Kids Birding, Astronomy, Owl Prowls, and a free day-long annual Fall Wildlife Festival and Plant Sale. Docent-guided bird tours are available. Over 300 bird species have been identified in the area. Plant and bird guides are available online.

Educational: MLAC works with local school districts and homeschool groups using the Nature of Learning place-based science program for grades 3—8. The program strengthens science skills and is aligned with state education standards. Hands-on activities relate to ecology, scientific observation, resource management, and citizenship. Water-related activities are emphasized. Title 1 schools are eligible for reduced rates. The San Antonio Water System offers a Mini-Grant Program for projects that educate pre-K–12 students on water issues and problems. Water-related field trips to MLAC are eligible.

A docent training program is offered.

Directions: Just minutes south of downtown San Antonio, the entrance gate is on Pleasanton Rd. Take Loop 410, exit 46 onto Moursund Blvd. and go south about 1 mile (Moursund becomes Pleasanton Rd.). The gate is on the left at 10750 Pleasanton Rd. The website includes a link to a printable map.

GPS Coordinates: Latitude: 29° 18.631`N     Longitude: 98° 30.125`W

The Mitchell Lake Audubon Center entrance

The Mitchell Lake Audubon Center

PINEY WOODS

The East Texas Piney Woods region is part of a larger mixed pine-hardwood forest system that extends into Texas from Oklahoma, Arkansas, and Louisiana. Pine trees prefer sandy, well-drained soils and ample rainfall.

Over the last 60 million years, 225 miles of sand, clay, and gravel sediment wedges, eroded from the continent by rivers, were deposited into the Gulf of Mexico. During this time span, this sediment dumping moved the Gulf coastline from Texarkana to Galveston. The northern part of the region, where the oldest rocks are found, has a rolling, hilly landscape due to alternating sequences of sandstones and shales. The harder sandstones form the ridges while the softer shales have been eroded by rivers and streams to form valleys. This hilliness lessens as you move toward the coast and younger sediments. Sandstone hardens with age and so resists erosion more than shale.

Average annual rainfall varies from 40 inches in the northwest to 56 inches in the southeast with no marked seasonal peaks. Temperatures are mild in the winter and humidity is high much of the time. Elevations range from 50 feet in the south on the coastal plain to 500 feet in the north.

Forests are not unbroken but form a mosaic of diverse, scattered habitats including small farms, upland grasslands and pastures, bald cypress and water tupelo swamps, bogs, bottomland hardwood forests, and extensive commercial pine plantations. The most famous of the cypress swamps in Texas are found in the shallow waters of Caddo Lake near Marshall. In the south near Beaumont, dense thickets of shrubs like gallberry, yaupon holly, and black titi along the drainages gave rise to the name Big Thicket. Part of what remains has been set aside as the Big Thicket National Preserve. In the mixed pine-hardwood forests oaks, elms, hickory, sweetgum and blackgum, ash, and hawthorns are the most common hardwoods. The pines include loblolly, shortleaf, and, mostly gone now, longleaf. The introduced slash pine has been widely grown in commercial plantations.

The fertile, well-watered floodplain soils of the region's rivers and streams support hardwood forests dominated by trees like water and willow oak, elm, ash, and sweetgum. These bottomland hardwood forests are perhaps the region's most valuable fish and wildlife habitats. The hardwoods have been subjected to increasing harvest pressure as the demand for pulp to make high-quality paper has risen. Also, the creation of large dams and reservoirs has drowned much bottomland habitat. Downstream from the dams the flood-plains are deprived of the annual overbank flooding the forests depend upon. The floodplain habitats dry out, and with the risk of flooding lessened, become more susceptible to development for agriculture, forestry, and other land uses. One of the promised "benefits" of most dams is downstream flood control.

Floodplain forests have economic values other than just timber produc-tion. The forests and swamps absorb floodwaters and release it slowly, thereby dampening flood crests and decreasing erosion and flood damage downstream. They also provide recreational opportunities like fishing, hunting, bird-watch-ing, and hiking that have economic value.

Pines have historically been the primary timber producing trees. Almost all the virgin timber has been logged at least once. Overharvest, along with suppression of natural fire (longleaf pine savanna is a fire adapted ecosystem) and damage to seedlings by free-ranging hogs, are the reasons the longleaf pine savannas of the entire southeastern U.S. are mostly gone. Longleaf pine savanna once dominated the southeastern part of the Piney Woods region. Some species that depended on the longleaf habitats, like the red-cockaded woodpecker, are now endangered.

An emerging threat to pine trees across the southern U.S. is a worsening of infestations by the southern pine beetle. The cause of these spreading infes-tations appears to be warming temperatures and other weather changes related to climate change due to global warming. Many pine trees have been lost to these infestations in recent years in East Texas. The dead trees provide fuel for wildfires.

Other industries, besides forestry, of importance to the region are livestock production and oil, gas, and lignite production. The East Texas oil field near Kilgore and Longview, discovered in 1930, is the largest in the lower 48 states and is still producing.

Clearcut logging in the Piney Woods

Figure 7 shows the distribution of facilities in the Piney Woods region.

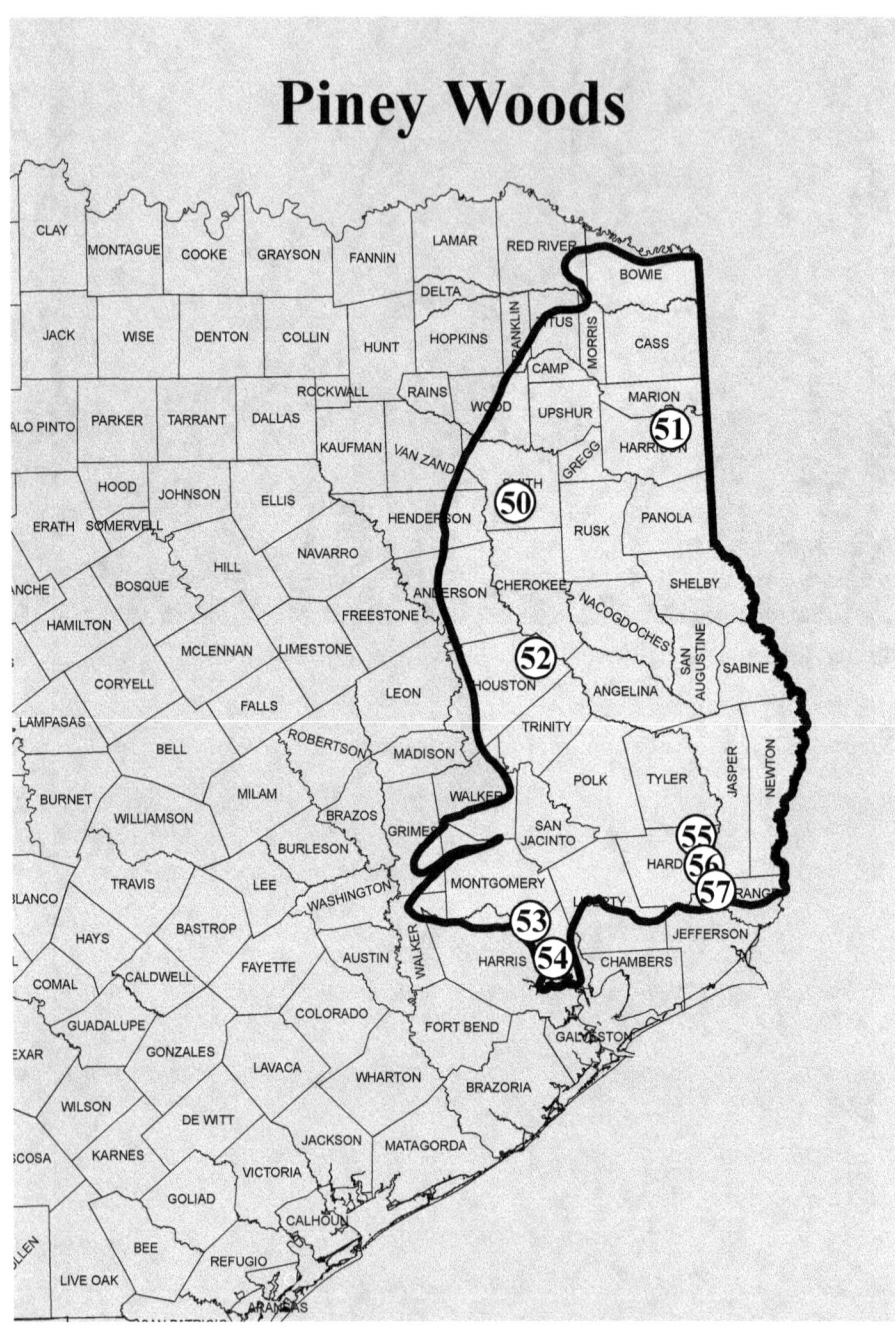

Figure 7—Facilities in the Piney Woods region

East Texas Ecological Education Center at Tyler (Nature Center)

11942 FM 848, Tyler, TX 75707

Owner: Texas Parks & Wildlife Dept.   **Size:** 82 acres

Contacts: Phone 903-566-1626 ext. 219

Website: http://www.tpwd.state.tx.us/huntwild/hunt/wma/find_a_wma/list/?id=59

Natural Region: Piney Woods

Major Ecosystem(s): Gilley Creek watershed; pine-hardwood forest; restored prairie

Overview: This former quail farm has 10 acres of grassland that is being restored to prairie. The forested areas are mostly fourth generation trees that have been cut over 3 times since the early 1800s. Three types of forest are present: dry upland pine, more moist upland hardwoods, and moist bottomland hardwoods. There is also a woodland pond that is stocked with fish. The Forest Loop Trail is 1 mile along spring-fed Quail Creek, a tributary of Gilley Creek.

The site has a VC with wheelchair access, indoor and outdoor classrooms, the Friendship Pavilion, and 2 sets of restrooms. It is open to the public Monday–Saturday on a group reservation basis. The East Texas Woods & Waters Foundation cooperates with TPWD in operating the facility. There is no entry fee.

Fun for Kids: Several fishing events for kids such as "Trails to Trout" are held at the fishing pond throughout the year. Hunter education classes and instructor training workshops are conducted each year.

Family Fun: The nature trail has an online brochure available ("Nature Trails of the Nature Center"). A working beehive display is located adjacent to the parking area.

Educational: This facility does not have permanent full-time staff. Programs and hikes are presented by teachers and group leaders visiting the facility. A nature trail guide, correlated to the numbered stations along the trails, can be downloaded from the website. This brochure describes plants as well as habitat types on the area. The trail along Quail Creek has a hands-on section. The facility is used as an outdoor classroom by local area colleges, ISDs, and civic groups.

Small acreage landowner workshops demonstrating various wildlife management strategies for small tracts of land are conducted periodically.

Directions: From Tyler, take Loop 323 to Spur 248 (southeast of Taylor). Go east on Spur 248 past the UT-Tyler campus to FM 848 (about 3 miles). Turn right on FM 848 and go about 1 mile.

GPS Coordinates: Latitude: 32° 18.485´N   Longitude: 95° 12.815´W

The East Texas Ecological Education Center at Tyler

The ETEEC at Tyler working beehive exhibit

Caddo Lake State Park & Wildlife Management Area

245 Park Rd. 2, Karnack, TX 75661

Owner: Texas Parks & Wildlife Dept.   **Size:** 8,489 acres

Contacts: Phone 903-679-3351; Fax 903-679-4006

Website: www.tpwd.state.tx.us/state-parks/caddo-lake

Natural Region: Piney Woods

Major Ecosystem(s): Caddo Lake; Cypress Bayou watershed; bald cypress-water tupelo swamp

Overview: Often called the only natural lake in Texas, an unglaciated region, it was dammed in the early 1900s after the discovery of oil. The lake originally formed when a massive log jam on the Red River backed water up into the Cypress Bayou watershed. This jam, known as the Great Raft of the Red River, was cleared for navigation in 1874.

The lake supports the most extensive bald cypress swamps in Texas. Much of the lake is a maze of sloughs, bayous, and ponds. The lake supports 71 species of fish and offers excellent fishing.

Fun for Kids: The VC features an interpretive center with exhibits, a self-guided nature trail, and a park store. There is a children's playground.

Family Fun: Commercial pontoon boat tours start in the park on weekends (March–November). They can be scheduled for other times by calling 903-930-0075. Canoes can be rented in the park daily (year-round). You can also bring your own canoe or kayak. Guided nature hikes, paddling tours, and other activities and instruction are offered. There are excellent fishing opportunities.

Educational: The interpretive center features exhibits on the history and ecology of Caddo Lake and the local Caddo Indians, as well as more than 2 miles of trails with a 0.5 mile self-guided nature trail.

Park staff gives regularly scheduled guided nature hikes, geocaching instruction, fishing instruction, bird-watching hikes, Friday evening Owl Prowls and bat programs, and paddling tours on Big Cypress Bayou.

Directions: From Karnack, go north 1 mile on SH 43 to FM 2198. Go east for 0.5 mile to Park Rd. 2. The park is 15 miles northeast of Marshall. The website includes a printable map.

GPS Coordinates: Latitude: 32° 40.713´ N   Longitude: 94° 10.526´ W

Caddo Lake State Park VC and Interpretive Center

Caddo Lake State Park Interpretive Center native peoples diorama

Lighted fishing pier in the swamp at Caddo Lake State Park

Treetops-in-the-Forest

CR 1175, Davy Crockett National Forest, Houston County, TX

Owner: Alternative Learning Environments, Inc. **Size:** 20 acres

Contacts: Phone 972-262-2816; E-mail form on website

Website: http://treetopsintheforest.org/

Natural Region: Piney Woods

Major Ecosystem(s): Neches River drainage basin (Big Slough Wilderness); upland hardwood, pine, and mixed pine-hardwood forest

Overview: Treetops-in-the-Forest sits on 20 pine-covered privately-owned acres in the Davy Crockett National Forest adjacent to the 3,455-acre Big Slough Wilderness. The Four C National Recreation Trail system can be accessed from the campus. The grounds include orienteering trails, a pond for fishing and aquatic studies, sustainability projects, child-built shelters, a labyrinth, and the main building where students sleep 4 to 6 per room. Austin, Houston, and Dallas/Fort Worth are about 3 to 4 hours away and participants are usually transported to the campus by their sponsoring schools or by parent carpools.

The regrowth forest is primarily shortleaf and loblolly pine with some hardwoods such as oak, hickory, and sweetgum. Southern pine beetles have killed many trees in this region.

Fun for Kids: Weeklong in-residence summer camps for elementary age kids are held in July and August. Scholarships are available for elementary age children of military families. A Junior Counselor Work Week is held in June. The area features a fishing pond, labyrinth, trails, teepee, and outdoor theater.

Family Fun: Programs for parents and young children include Treetops Tiny Tots, a parent education program encouraging nature experiences during infancy. A Day in the Woods is a free program for preschool children and their parents or grandparents to spend a day at Treetops exploring the natural world together. The Families in the Forest program invites 4 families (4 to 6 members each) to spend 4 "seasonal" weekends in the forest at Treetops.

Educational: Weeklong in-residence sessions for organized school groups include a range of environmental topics related to the arts, sciences, and humanities. The curriculum for public schools includes content aligned with state education standards. Programs for various special focus groups may be scheduled by request for 10 or more students.

Programs for teachers include various workshops and retreats. Individual teacher professional development retreats for CPE credit can also be scheduled. Some curriculum development resources are available for use by teachers.

Directions: From Dallas, take I-45 south. Exit onto SH 7E at Centerville. Go east on 7E through Centerville, Crockett, and Kennard. Go left on FM 227 at Ratcliff and veer right onto the dirt road (CR 1165). Follow the dirt road to the intersection with CR 1175 and go left on CR 1175. Treetops is the second gate on the right.

GPS Coordinates: Latitude: 31°26.988′ N   Longitude: 95°07.738′ W

The bunkhouse at Treetops-in-the-Forest

The fishing pond at Treetops-in-the-Forest

The outdoor theatre at Treetops-in-the-Forest

53 Jesse H. Jones Park & Nature Center

20634 Kenswick Dr., Humble, TX 77338

Owner: Harris County Precinct 4   **Size:** 300+ acres

Contacts: Phone 281-446-8588; Fax 281-446-8832; E-mail JJP@hcp4.net

Website: www.hcp4.net/jones/index.htm

Natural Region: Piney Woods

Major Ecosystem(s): Spring Creek floodplain

Overview: Spring Creek is a tributary of the West Fork of the San Jacinto River. This site is on the southern edge of the Piney Woods region. The creek has white sand beaches with mature bald cypress in swamps and sloughs. The floodplain supports mixed pine-hardwood bottomland forest.

There are over 9 miles of all-weather trails with interpretive signage, boardwalks, and wildlife viewing blinds. The nature center has environmental displays, dioramas, mounted specimens, and native live snake and frog displays. Wildlife-attracting native landscape plant beds surround the center. The center also features the Redbud Hill Homestead and Akokisa Indian Village. There is a limited recycling drop-off program.

Fun for Kids: Kids In Action programs include fishing and summer nature camps for kids ages 5–12 in June and July. Scouting programs include badge workshops, Try-Its, naturalist-led talks and forest tours, as well as service projects.

Family Fun: There are 4 annual festivals, such as Nature Fest, and free weekend programs on environmental and nature topics. Pavilion, picnic area, and playground facilities are available. Pontoon boat, canoe, and bicycle tours, as well as canoe training workshops can be scheduled.

Educational: Guided field trips and group tours feature programs on nature or pioneer history. Special programs emphasize native plants, animals, and habitats as well as geology, canoe training, hunter education, and other topics. There are programs for all grades and ages. An environmental outreach program, including a speaker's guide, for schools, libraries, and organizations is free and is aligned with state education standards.

Directions: From Houston, go north about 19 miles on US 59. Go west about 2 miles on FM 1960 to Kenswick Dr. Go north 1 mile to the entrance. The website includes a printable map.

GPS Coordinates: Latitude: 30° 01.360´ N   Longitude: 95° 17.657´ W

The Jesse II. Jones Park & Nature Center

The Redbud Hill Homestead at Jesse H. Jones

The Akokisa Indian Village at Jesse H. Jones

Sheldon Lake State Park & Environmental Learning Center

15315 Beaumont Highway (Business 90) @ Park Rd. 138, Houston, TX 77049

Owner: Texas Parks & Wildlife Dept.   **Size:** SP—2,800 acres; ELC—40 acres

Contacts: Phone 281-456-2800; Fax 281-456-8456; E-mail sheldonlake@tpwd.state.tx.us

Website: www.tpwd.state.tx.us/state-parks/sheldon-lake

Natural Region: Piney Woods

Major Ecosystem(s): Lower San Jacinto River watershed

Overview: Sheldon Reservoir is on Carpenter's Bayou, a tributary of Buffalo Bayou, which runs into the lower San Jacinto River. Floodplain forests include cypress swamp, bottomland hardwoods, and mixed pine-hardwood on the higher areas. The reservoir includes about 400 acres of marsh and swamp. The ELC has converted the ponds of an old fish hatchery into an outdoor aquatic classroom complex with accessible nature trails, fishing ponds, aquatic study stations, etc. The 61-foot-tall John Jacob Observation Tower is ADA-compliant and provides views of Sheldon Lake, the prairie and wetland restoration complex, downtown Houston, and the surrounding industrial complex. There is a wildscape demonstration garden with native plants and environmental sustainability demos (green building/alternative energy).

This facility is located on the northeastern edge of Houston. There is no entrance fee.

Fun for Kids: The reservoir is open to public fishing from dawn until dusk.

Family Fun: Free weekend catch-and-release "Family Fishing" for kids is offered. All trails and facilities, including the observation tower, are ADA-compliant.

Educational: Educational field trips are available for school classes and other groups. Programs include fishing, aquatic ecology, nature discovery walks, and environmental sustainability demonstrations. Programs can be adapted to individual groups and detailed guides linked to state educational standards are available for each activity. The ELC Pond Center includes aquatic study stations, habitat restoration, and recreational facilities.

Service learning projects involving hands-on natural resource field activities such as forest, wetland, or prairie restoration are available to schools, scouts, and corporate groups.

Directions: From the I-610E/I-10 interchange, take US 90 (Crosby Freeway) to Miller Rd 3. Turn left on Miller Rd. 3 and go 1 mile. Turn right on Business 90 (Beaumont Hwy) and go east 0.25 mile to Park Rd. 138. Turn left over the railroad tracks to the park entrance. The website includes a printable map.

GPS Coordinates: Latitude: 29° 51.315´ N   Longitude: 95° 09.539´ W

A classroom at Sheldon Lake State Park

An aquatic study station at Sheldon Lake State Park

The John Jacob Observation Tower at Sheldon Lake State Park

55 Roy E. Larsen Sandyland Sanctuary

4208 SH 327 (P.O. Box 909), Silsbee, TX 77656

Owner: The Nature Conservancy of Texas   **Size:** 5,654 acres

Contacts: Phone 409-385-0445

Website: http://www.nature.org/ourinitiatives/regions/northamerica/united-states/texas/placesweprotect/roy-e-larsen-sandyland-sanctuary.xml

Natural Region: Piney Woods

Major Ecosystem(s): Longleaf pine savanna; Village Creek and floodplain

Overview: This site is in Hardin County about 20 miles north of Beaumont in the heart of the Big Thicket. It supports one of the last remaining areas of long-leaf pine savanna in Texas. It has very high biological diversity and several community types on the ancient alluvial deposits of Village Creek. Longleaf pine is found on the sandy uplands. Fire management is used to maintain the longleaf pine savanna habitat.

The floodplain supports baygall and sphagnum bog communities where the Neches River once formed sloughs and channels. Floodplain forests include water oak, sweetgum, willow, and river birch. Intermediate elevations support forests of American beech, southern magnolia, and loblolly pine. All virgin timber in the region was logged by 1930 and the forests today are second- or third-growth forests. The site connects the Big Thicket National Preserve on its north and south boundaries along the Village Creek corridor.

Fun for Kids: There are 6 miles of trails including a self-guided interpretive trail.

Family Fun: An 8.5 mile stretch of Village Creek meanders through the preserve and canoe trips can be arranged with local vendors. The creek has no water control measures so water levels can change rapidly. Eastex Canoe Trails (www.eastexcanoes.com) is a good source of real-time water level conditions on the creek.

Education: The area has 6 miles of trails. A self-guided interpretive trail guide is available for a 1-mile section of the trail system. Interpretive programs are available upon request for groups of 10 or more.

Individuals and groups, for example Texas Master Naturalists, may volunteer to help with a variety of science and stewardship work such as habitat management for rare plants, bobwhite quail, etc. The preserve is used by several local academic institutions as a natural classroom for field labs and research.

Directions: From Beaumont, go north on US 96 to Silsbee. Turn west for 2.5 miles on SH 327 to the entrance. The canoe trail starts where FM 418 crosses Village Creek. The website includes printable maps.

GPS Coordinates: Latitude: 30° 20.919`N     Longitude: 94° 14.168`W

The Roy E. Larsen Sandyland Sanctuary parking area and trailhead

An interpretive nature trail at Roy E. Larsen

Big Thicket National Preserve

6102 FM 420, Kountze, TX 77625

Owner: National Park Service   **Size:** 105,684 acres

Contacts: Phone 409-951-6700; Fax 409-951-6714; E-mail form on website

Website: www.nps.gov/bith

Natural Region: Piney Woods

Major Ecosystem(s): Neches River floodplain; coastal flatwoods (mixed pine-hardwoods)

Overview: The preserve consists of 9 upland and 6 riparian corridor units. The riparian corridors along the Neches River and several tributaries feature bottomland hardwood forests and cypress swamp habitats. Upland units include mixed pine-hardwood forests, meadows, and bogs.

This region has high biological diversity because it is located at the convergence of two major natural areas: the Piney Woods and Gulf Coast Prairies and Marshes. Also, during the last Ice Age, the southern end of the Great Plains extended into this region, and some influences and components from that ecosystem remain today. Entry and all activities are free (call 409-951-6700 for reservations).

Fun for Kids: Junior Ranger and "Webrangers" programs (www.nps.gov/webrangers) are offered. The VC features a bookstore, orientation films, interactive interpretive exhibits, and a hands-on Discovery Room.

Family Fun: Rangers lead monthly two-hour Neches River cruises on the *Cardinal* (409-651-5326), a pontoon boat operated by Lamar University (LU charges a fee) which is also available for school programs. There are 9 hiking trails ranging from 0.25 mile wheelchair-accessible to 17 miles long.

Educational: A wide variety of curriculum-based education and free interpretive programs for pre-K–12 are offered. Field trips, classroom visits, and interpretive programs can be tailored to meet the goals of your group. Teacher workshops (such as the Project WILD series) are offered from time to time and can be scheduled by request. The GLOBE ecosystem analysis program for students combines field, lab, and classroom studies.

Directions: From I-10 in Beaumont, take US Hwy 69/287 north. Eight miles north of Kountze, take FM 420 east and follow the signs to the VC. The website includes a printable map.

GPS Coordinates: Latitude: 30°27.434'N   Longitude: 94°23.162'W

The Big Thicket National Preserve VC

Interactive exhibits in the Big Thicket VC

57 Village Creek State Park

8854 Park Rd. 74 (off Alma Dr.), Lumberton, TX 77657

Owner: Texas Parks & Wildlife Dept.   **Size:** 2,500 acres

Contacts: Phone 409-755-7322; Fax 409-755-3183

Website: http://www.tpwd.state.tx.us/state-parks/village-creek

Natural Region: Piney Woods

Major Ecosystem(s): Big Thicket; Lower Neches River floodplain

Overview: VCSP is in Hardin County 10 miles north of Beaumont. Village Creek, in the heart of what remains of the Big Thicket, is a free-flowing stream that rises near the Alabama-Coushatta Indian Reservation and flows southeast 69 miles to the Neches River. The heavily forested park features bottomland trees such as bald cypress and water tupelo, river birch, mayhaw, and yaupon, as well as baygalls and backwater sloughs. More than 200 species of birds are native to the Big Thicket.

Hurricanes Rita (2005) and Ike (2008) damaged over 600 acres of trees in the park and those areas will require a long time to recover; even with a reforestation plan in place.

Fun for Kids: The Saturday nature programs feature a variety of topics on the Big Thicket ecosystem. Facilities include a children's playground, 8-person cabin, group pavilion, camping facilities, and 8 miles of trails for hiking, mountain biking, and nature study.

Family Fun: Canoe rentals are available from nearby local outfitters. The park is part of the Village Creek Paddling Trail. Texas Outdoor Family Workshops are offered occasionally. The area provides exceptional bird-watching opportunities. There is a land navigation map and compass course.

Educational: Tours, interpretive, and educational programs are offered year-round. Programs include nature trail hikes, self-guided trails, night hikes, slide shows, and campfire talks. Tours, programs, and school field trips are also available by request.

Directions: From Beaumont, take US Hwy 69/96 north and take the Mitchell Rd. exit. Go about 0.4 mile on the access road and turn east onto Mitchell Rd. Then turn immediately north (left) onto FM 3513 (Village Creek Parkway). Go about 2 miles and turn east (right) on Alma Dr. Cross the railroad tracks (veer to left) and go 0.5 mile to the park.

GPS Coordinates: Latitude: 30° 14.801'N   Longitude: 94° 10.854'W

The Village Creek State Park entrance

A children's playground and interpretive nature trail at Village Creek State Park

SOUTH TEXAS BRUSH COUNTRY

If you drop down off the south edge of the Edwards Plateau and cross the Balcones Fault zone, you come onto the South Texas plains. These rolling plains sit atop bands of sandstone and shale that were deposited by rivers and streams into the Gulf of Mexico over the last 60 million years. These bands of sedimentary rock become younger as you travel from the original Gulf shoreline near San Antonio toward the present Gulf coast. The topography of the plains is rolling with ridges and valleys. The sandstone ridges are more resistant to erosion than the shales, which have eroded to form the drainages. As you approach the coast, you go from the rolling terrain of the Tertiary period outcrops to the younger, very flat Pleistocene (2 million to 100,000 years ago) coastal plain deposits. The Lower Rio Grande Valley (LRGV), from upstream around Roma to Brownsville, consists of dark, fertile floodplain soils deposited by the Rio Grande during the last 2 million years. The floodplain has younger, moister, more fertile soils than the brush country.

Average annual rainfall varies from 18 inches in the west to 32 inches in the northeast with peaks in the spring and fall. Summer temperatures are high as are evaporation rates, especially in the west. In the LRGV, winter temperatures are very mild. Elevations range from near sea level near the coast to 1,000 feet in the west.

In the mid-1800s, the South Texas plains were covered by grasslands with scattered groves of trees like large mesquites in low areas and along streams and rivers. Overgrazing and the suppression of natural grassland fires allowed mesquite and other thorny brush like acacias, prickly pear, blackbrush, and granjeno to invade the grasslands. Thorny brush is not very palatable to cattle; however, the brush is nutritious deer browse and has helped make white-tailed deer hunting economically important in South Texas. Livestock grazing is the principal agricultural industry.

The LRGV is 1 of 2 extensions of the subtropics, the other is south Florida into the continental U.S. Evergreen floodplain forests of Texas palmetto (sabal palm), Texas ebony, anacua, and cedar elm once grew on moist river and resaca (oxbow lakes and abandoned river channels) terraces. On the higher, drier parts of the floodplain, subtropical brush including mesquite, snakeeyes, lotebush, brasil, and granjeno were once found. Most of the forests and brush of the LRGV have been cleared for agriculture and urban development; however, many subtropical species of birds and mammals found nowhere else in the U.S. can be seen in the LRGV. In fact, bird-watchers that come from all over the world make up a very important segment of the economy in the LRGV. So do the "winter Texans" or "snow birds" who are attracted by the climate as well as bird-watching and other recreational opportunities.

By the time the Rio Grande reaches the LRGV, its waters consist entirely of irrigation return flows and effluents from wastewater treatment plants and industries. Therefore, it is not surprising that water quality as well as quantity are both problematic. At times, the river ceases to flow into the Gulf. The productivity of the estuary has been damaged by the curtailed freshwater inflows.

The rich floodplain soils combined with mild winters and irrigation water from the river have made the LRGV one of the most important fruit and vegetable growing regions in the nation.

The Texas Parks and Wildlife Department and the U.S. Fish and Wildlife Service along with The Nature Conservancy and the National Audubon Society have acquired land and tried to reestablished brush habitat for endangered species like the ocelot and jaguarundi.

Remnant sabal palm trees at the Sabal Palm Sanctuary near Brownsville

Figure 8 shows the distribution of facilities in the South Texas Brush Country region.

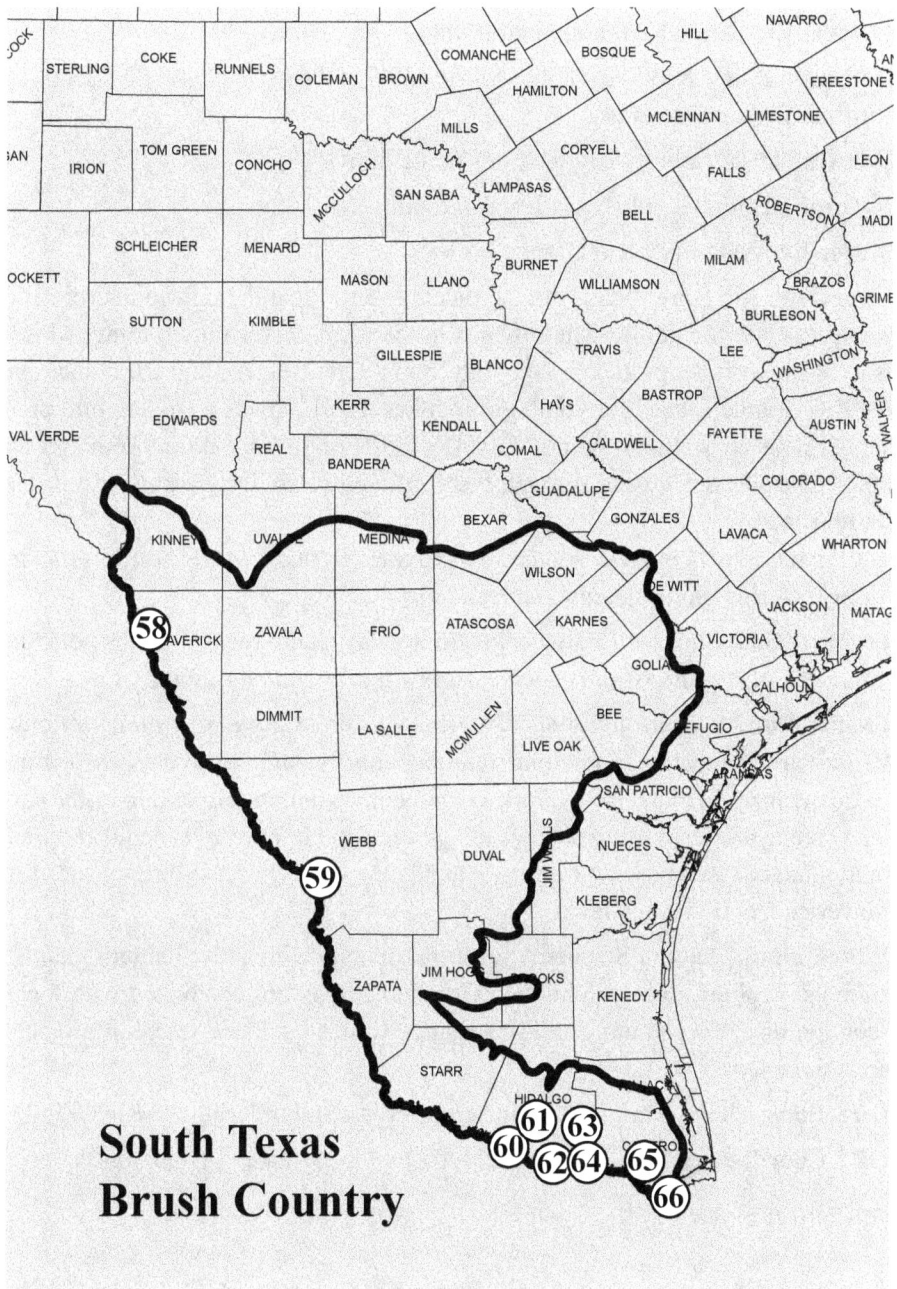

Figure 8—Facilities in the South Texas Brush Country region

58 Rio Bravo Nature Center

1345 Simpson Dr. (private home), Eagle Pass, TX 78852

Owner: Rio Bravo N.C. Foundation, Inc.

Contacts: Phone 830-773-1836; Mobile 830-776-0638; E-mail wild-friends@ RioBravoNatureCenter.org

Website: http://riobravonaturectr.org/home.html

Natural Region: South Texas Brush Country

Major Ecosystem(s): Rio Grande Valley

Overview: Rio Bravo NC is not a typical center in that there is no interpretive center open to the public. The office is in the local Girl Scout building, which is used for workshops and ecology day camp activities. An 800-acre ranch on the Rio Grande is used for youth group hikes. RBNC owns a 10-acre bird preserve on the river; this is part of TPWD's Heart of Texas Wildlife Trail (West) #002. The site is accessed through the north end of Shelby Park using Border Patrol roads.

As far as I know, this is the only program in this part of the Rio Grande Valley offering environmental education to the public.

Fun for Kids: Summer Ecology Adventure Day Camp (ages 7–13) is held the first week of August. Youth canoe classes are offered at the County Lake.

Family Fun: Various activities centering on the migration of monarch butterflies are conducted, including public butterfly tagging events (Monarch Extravaganza) held in Shelby Park in October. Monarch migration cluster-site maps are available. Group canoe trips on the Rio Grande are scheduled on an individual contract basis. A birding list and map of easy access birding sites for Maverick County is available.

Educational: Outdoor Science Adventures dealing with native habitats, plants, animals, geology, and regional Rio Grande ecology are conducted with local scouting and other youth groups. Volunteer citizen science research projects are conducted.

Directions: Shelby Park is at Main St. and Ryan St. bordering the Rio Grande.

GPS Coordinates: Latitude: 28° 42.490˙N   Longitude: 100° 30.454˙W

Float trip on the Rio Grande (photo courtesy of Carol Cullar of the Rio Bravo Nature Center)

Tagging monarchs at Shelby Park in Eagle Pass (photo courtesy of Carol Cullar of the Rio Bravo Nature Center)

58 Lamar Bruni Vergara Environmental Science Center

Laredo Community College, West End Washington St., Laredo, TX 78040

Owner: Laredo Community College

Contacts: Phone 956-764-5701; Fax 956-764-5929; E-mail lbvesc@laredo. edu

Website: http://www.laredo.edu/cms/LCC/Instruction/Divisions/ Arts_and_Humanities/LBV_Environmental_Science_Center/ LBV_Environmental_Science_Center/

Natural Region: South Texas Brush Country

Major Ecosystem(s): Rio Grande Valley

Overview: LBVESC is on the north edge of the Laredo Community College (LCC) campus close to the Rio Grande. It functions as a living science laboratory for LCC students and as a center for science education for the region's pre-K–12 schoolchildren. There are several water areas with live specimens native to the Rio Grande ecosystem, growing areas for native vegetation, wildlife diorama displays, a wetlands demonstration project, and the adjacent Paso del Indio Nature Trail. The plantings include a cactus garden, wildflower hill, and South Texas brush.

As far as I know, this is the only facility in the Laredo area offering environmental education to the public.

Fun for Kids: Various summer day camps are offered for kids ages 4–15. Four ponds feature native fish and turtles, and a wetland area for young alligators. Indoor aquaria and terraria feature fish, amphibians, reptiles, and rodents.

Family Fun: Special events such as Earth Day Festival (spring) and Dia del Rio (fall) are offered. There is the Paso del Indio Nature Trail.

Educational: Local public and private school classes for pre-K–12 participate in the eco-curriculum through instructional tours scheduled on weekdays throughout the school year. These guided classes vary from 1 to 5 hours in length and may include hands-on activities and trail walks.

Directions: From the main campus (Fort McIntosh campus), drive down Washington St. overpass, turn right on Victoria St., turn right on Sherman, then left on Taylor Rd. The college website has a printable campus map.

GPS Coordinates: Latitude: 27° 30.530´N   Longitude: 99° 31.359´ W

The Lamar Bruni Vergara Environmental Science Center

The Paso Del Indio nature trail at Lamar Bruni Vergara

The World Birding Center

The World Birding Center (WBC) is a cooperative venture of the Texas Parks and Wildlife Department, the U.S. Fish and Wildlife Service, and 9 LRGV communities. The WBC consists of 9 sites that stretch from Roma inland to South Padre Island on the Gulf. The facilities described below (60, 61, 64, 65) offer exceptional educational and recreational opportunities for both school groups and families.

60 Bentsen-Rio Grande Valley State Park

2800 S. Bentsen Palm Dr. (FM 2062), Mission, TX 78572

Owner: Texas Parks & Wildlife Dept.   **Size:** 762 acres

Contacts: Phone 956-584-9156; Fax 956-584-9126; E-mail mailto:George. Cortez@tpwd.texas.gov

Website: www.theworldbirdingcenter.com/Bentsen.html

Natural Region: South Texas Brush Country

Major Ecosystem(s): Lower Rio Grande Valley

Overview: This park is the headquarters of the World Birding Center. Habitats include riparian and thorn scrub forest, resaca (river oxbow lakes and old channels) wetlands, and revegetated agricultural fields. There are bird and butterfly feeding stations throughout the park, three wheelchair-accessible bird blinds, 3 observation decks, and a 2-story wheelchair-accessible observation tower. There are 8 miles of trails and a daily open-air tram service that moves people around the park. Bicycle rentals are available.

The VC buildings incorporate many green design features including a rainwater collection system that feeds watering troughs that attract birds and butterflies to the gardens.

Fun for Kids: There is a gift shop and bilingual exhibit hall in the VC. There are 8 miles of trails and an open-air tram ride. Bicycle rentals are available.

Family Fun: The La Familia Nature Center, located just inside the park gates, is a learning center where exhibits and displays in both Spanish and English change throughout the year. Families and other park visitors can learn about resident wildlife through interactive exhibits, and find out about the latest wildlife sightings.

Educational: Programs are aligned with state education standards and can be customized with advance notice. A variety of standard, guided field trips with hands-on activities are offered. These include programs with birds, butterflies and other insects, owls, wetlands and woodlands, etc. Outreach efforts include in-class presentations, career days, and other school programs.

Also offered are teacher continuing education workshops and environmental education programs such as Project WILD. Teachers can check out supplies to use for Project WILD and Aquatic WILD classroom activities. Service learning projects are customized to incorporate learning objectives with projects that benefit the park and community.

Directions: From Mission, take West Expressway 83 to Bentsen Palm Dr. Go south on Bentsen Palm to WBC Headquarters at the park. The website includes a printable map.

GPS Coordinates: Latitude: 26° 11.170ʹ N   Longitude: 98° 22.734ʹ W

The World Birding Center headquarters at Bentsen-Rio Grande Valley State Park

The La Familia Nature Center at Bentsen-Rio Grande Valley State Park

Quinta Mazatlan

600 Sunset Dr., McAllen, TX 78503

Owner: City of McAllen   **Size:** 15 acres

Contacts: Phone 956-681-3370; Fax 956-681-3379; E-mail form on website

Website: www.quintamazatlan.com

Natural Region: South Texas Brush Country

Major Ecosystem(s): Lower Rio Grande Valley (urban)

Overview: Quinta Mazatlan ("country estate" in Spanish) is the McAllen wing of the World Birding Center. This old country estate, dating from the 1930s, is one of the largest adobe homes in Texas. Formal tropical gardens, enhanced with native plants, serve as a backyard bird habitat demonstration. Wild Tamaulipan thorn forest has been enhanced with water and bird feeding stations.

This urban sanctuary features walking trails with bird feeding stations, hummingbird lane, a migratory bird meadow, native butterfly garden, cactus garden, nature exhibits, and nature art gallery. There is also a Forest Sculpture Trail of bronzes telling the story of native wildlife featuring Wildcat Lane.

Fun for Kids: Nature Discovery Camp is a summer day camp for kids ages 6–12. A variety of scout and youth programs for both Boy and Girl Scouts (all levels) meet all the requirements for many badges. The Children's Discovery

Center deck overlooks a wildlife pond. There are natural playscape areas with a Mesquite Cookie Trail and Boulder Hill.

Family Fun: A wide variety of programs, tours (Woodland Walkabout, Garden of Eatin', Stroll thru History), and special events are available including the Nature Speaker series on Thursday evenings for adults and families. The annual Earth Day Festival (VIDA VERDE) is held in April. There is an educational gift store and nature art gallery.

A Backyard Habitat Stewardship program is offered.

Educational: The School Science Series features educational field trips aligned with state education standards and emphasizing unique South Texas animals, plants, and habitats. These programs offer both indoor and outdoor lessons.

Online resources for teachers and group leaders include pre- and post-visit activity sheets, evaluation forms, field trip registration forms, etc.

Directions: In McAllen, take W. Expressway 83 to 10th St. exit. Go south on S. 10th St. and turn left (east) on Sunset Dr. Quinta Mazatlan is at the end of Sunset Dr. Park outside the big brown gates. The website includes a printable map.

GPS Coordinates: Latitude: 26° 10.610´N   Longitude: 98° 13.894´ W

The Quinta Mazatlan adobe house

Inside the Discovery Center at Quinta Mazatlan

62 Santa Ana National Wildlife Refuge

3325 Green Jay Rd., Alamo, TX 78516

Owner: U.S. Fish and Wildlife Service   **Size:** 2,088 acres

Contacts: Phone 956-784-7500; Fax 956-787-8338; E-mail mailto:Christine_ Donald@fws.gov

Website: www.fws.gov/refuge/Santa_Ana/

Natural Region: South Texas Brush Country

Major Ecosystem(s): Lower Rio Grande Valley

Overview: The refuge is a remnant island of subtropical thorn forest that once dominated the area. The riparian woodlands provide habitat for 400 bird species and about half of all butterfly species found in North America. The refuge has 12 miles of foot trails and access roads. Chachalaca trail is wheelchair accessible. During the winter, roving naturalists and guides assist visitors.

Fun for Kids: There is a bookstore and displays in the VC. An interpretive tram leaves the VC three times daily from Thanksgiving to May.

Family Fun: The refuge lends binoculars to visitors, along with maps, bird lists, and trail guides. The Friends of the Santa Ana NWR (956-783-6117), a non-profit organization, conducts seasonal canoe trips on the Rio Grande along the refuge and the Arroyo Colorado. There is a 7-mile wildlife auto drive.

Educational: Refuge staff and volunteers give free interpretive tours and talks. Talks and displays feature the wildlife and plants of the LRGV. The interpretive tram ride provides an introduction not only to the refuge but also to the LRGV.

Environmental education programs for all schools and grades are available upon request year-round. Call for more information.

Directions: From McAllen, take Hwy 83 east to Alamo. Turn south on FM 907 and go 7.5 miles. At Hwy 281 (Old Military Hwy) turn left and go 0.25 mile. The refuge is on the south side of the road. The website has a link to a printable map.

GPS Coordinates: Latitude: 26° 05.100ʹN   Longitude: 98° 08.068ʹW

Kids' activities at the Santa Ana National Wildlife Refuge VC

The Santa Ana NWR tram ride

Trails at the Santa Ana NWR

Valley Nature Center

301 South Border Ave./P.O. Box 8125, Weslaco, TX 78599

Owner: Valley Nature Center   **Size:** 6 acres

Contacts: Phone 956-969-2475; Fax 956-969-9915;
E-mail info@valleynaturecenter.org

Website: http://valleynaturecenter.org/

Natural Region: South Texas Brush Country

Major Ecosystem(s): Lower Rio Grande Valley

Overview: This facility features a wide variety of LRGV native plants and associated animals. The one-mile trail includes plants native to LRGV habitats including remnant sabal palm forest, coastal lomas (clay dunes), and Chihuahuan thorn forest. The facility features three cactus gardens, large butterfly gardens, several small ponds, a quarter-acre wetland with a boardwalk, and a native plant nursery that is open to the public. An 8,400-sq.-ft. environmental education center is scheduled for completion in 2013. Good birding and butterfly watching are available. VNC operates the interpretive tram at Santa Ana National Wildlife Refuge.

Fun for Kids: The exhibit hall features interactive displays and live animals. There is a Kids' Nature Club, a Kids' Birding Team, and Kids' summer nature camps.

Family Fun: A variety of special family nature events and programs are held. Some are continuous. Birding field trips are offered. The gift shop features South Texas books, etc. There is a 1-mile trail with ponds, a wetland and boardwalk, and butterfly gardens.

Educational: Guided school field trips, including joint field trips with Estero Llano Grande State Park that last all day and send students to both facilities, feature native plants and animals. Prepared curricula for teachers can be downloaded from the website.

Classes for adults and children feature South Texas natural history. VNC offers teacher training for CPE credit to individual teachers and teacher in-services to school districts.

Directions: From US 83 in Weslaco, turn south on Westgate Blvd., then east on Business 83, then south on Border Ave. Turn left into Gibson City Park and go through the parking lot to the back. The website includes a printable map.

GPS Coordinates: Latitude: 26° 09.530˙ N   Longitude: 97° 59.862˙ W

The Valley Nature Center's old VC

Chachalacas at a feeding station at the Valley Nature Center

The new environmental education center under construction in 2013 at the Valley Nature Center

Estero Llano Grande State Park

3301 S. International Blvd. (FM 1015), Weslaco, TX 78596

Owner: Texas Parks and Wildlife Dept.   **Size:** 230 acres

Contacts: Phone 956-565-3919; Fax 956-565-2864; E-mail mailto:martha. garcia@tpwd.state.tx.us

Website: www.theworldbirdingcenter.com/estero.html

Natural Region: South Texas Brush Country

Major Ecosystem(s): Lower Rio Grande Valley

Overview: Estero Llano Grande ("great estuary plain" in Spanish) is the Weslaco wing of the World Birding Center. It includes classic LRGV habitats—riparian woodlands and thorn scrub—and also features the most wetlands of any WBC unit. The large resaca is actually part of the Arroyo Colorado, an old channel of the Rio Grande. Former agricultural fields have been converted to wetlands including a nesting island.

The VC includes a park store, viewing deck, and classroom/meeting room. Over three miles of trails feature boardwalks, an observation deck, water features, and a pavilion. Camp Thicket is a large overnight group camping facility used for retreats, training, parties, etc. It features various sleeping arrangements, kitchens, dining halls, and other amenities. Facilities and programs are accessible to special needs visitors.

Fun for Kids: Electric tram nature tours run every Sunday afternoon, and can be scheduled at other times.

Family Fun: Special events include family campouts and Texas Outdoor Family Workshops. A varied array of programs for families and school groups are offered. Guided tours feature birds, butterflies and other insects, and nature walks.

Educational: School field trips include eight designed programs that can be customized with advance notice. All field trips involve hands-on activities. Joint field trips with the Valley Nature Center last all day and send students to both parks. An outreach program brings park staff to the school classroom. All school programs are aligned with state education standards. Workshops to help teachers prepare students for state science testing are offered. Special events include Teacher's Appreciation Day.

Directions: From Weslaco, take East Expressway 83 to FM 1015. Go south on FM 1015 crossing Business 83 and Mile 6 North. Look for the WBC entrance on the east side of FM 1015 before reaching Mile 5 North. The website includes a printable map.

GPS Coordinates: Latitude: 26° 07.631' N   Longitude: 97° 57.497' W

The Estero Llano Grande State Park VC from the boardwalk

65 Resaca de la Palma State Park

1000 New Carmen Rd. (off Hwy 281 or FM 1732), Brownsville, TX 78521

Owner: Texas Parks & Wildlife Dept.   **Size:** 1,200 acres

Contacts: Phone 956-350-2920; Fax 956-350-3814; E-mail mailto:pablo.dey-turbe@tpwd.state.tx.us

Website: www.theworldbirdingcenter.com/Resaca.html

Natural Region: South Texas Brush Country

Major Ecosystem(s): Lower Rio Gande Valley

Overview: Resaca de la Palma ("oxbow lake of the palms" in Spanish) is a reference to the once more extensive groves of sabal palm trees in the LRGV. The largest tract of native habitats in the World Birding Center network, the natural levees of the resaca support riparian woodlands and marsh vegetation. The drier areas support thorn scrub.

The VC has a park store and leads to 6 miles of trails (accessed by walking or biking), 4 decks that overlook 4 miles of resaca, and a 3-mile tram loop through the park. Some trails are special needs accessible. Bicycles and binoculars can be rented.

Fun for Kids: Junior Ranger camps are 4-day summer camps for kids in June and July.

Family Fun: Guided tours/programs include Family Nature Night, night hikes, bird walks, butterfly/dragonfly walks, and plant walks. Customized nature programs for any group are available upon request. Special events include Earth Day Celebration in April, Green Holiday Festival at Christmas, and Welcome Back Winter Texans in November.

Educational: School field trips emphasize birds, other wildlife, and the five habitats found in the park. Programs are aligned with state education standards and can be customized.

Directions: From Expressway 77/83, exit at Olmito and take FM 1732 for 2.5 miles. Turn left at New Carmen Rd. and go 1.5 miles. At the end of the pavement, turn left to enter the park. The website includes a printable map.

GPS Coordinates: Latitude: 25° 59.782´ N   Longitude: 97° 34.287´ W

The Resaca de la Palma State Park VC

A boardwalk on the resaca at Resaca de la Palma State Park

Sabal Palm Sanctuary

8435 Southmost Rd., Brownsville, TX 78523

Operator: Gorgas Science Foundation   **Owner:** National Audubon Society

Size: 557 acres

Contacts: Phone 956-541-8034; E-mail form on website

Website: www.sabalpalmsanctuary.org

Natural Region: South Texas Brush Country

Major Ecosystem(s): Lower Rio Grande Valley

Overview: Sabal palm groves were once quite common on the lower Rio Grande delta and extended for about 80 miles upstream from the Gulf. Today, only remnants of this forest remain, with this site being one of the best examples. This subtropical ecosystem is home to many native plants and animals that reach the northernmost limits of their Mexican range and do not occur elsewhere in the U.S. The site has 3 miles of nature trails with wildlife viewing areas, photo blinds, and elevated wetland boardwalks. Some are wheelchair accessible.

Also on site is the historical Rabb Plantation Home. Built in 1891, it is one of the last remaining plantation homes in the region. It became the new VC in summer 2013.

Fun for Kids: A LIVE Bird Feeder Cam can be accessed through the website.

Family Fun: Birding, nature, and historical tours by appointment for 8 or more are offered seasonally. Special events, wildlife presentations, and workshops are offered occasionally.

Educational: Special tours and activities for school and community groups are by appointment.

Directions: From US 77/83 in Brownsville, exit onto International Blvd. and go east. After 0.75 mile, turn right onto Southmost Rd. (FM 1419). Continue on Southmost Rd. for 6 miles; look for the entrance sign on the right. The website includes a printable map.

GPS Coordinates: Latitude: 25° 51.514˙N   Longitude: 97° 25.042˙W

Bird-watchers at the Sabal Palm Sanctuary office

Bird-watchers in a large blind at Sabal Palm Sanctuary

The Rabb Plantation became the new Sabal Palm Sanctuary VC in 2013

GULF COAST PRAIRIES & MARSHES/ COASTAL SAND PLAIN

The Texas Gulf coastal plain is over 360 miles long and 50 to 100 miles wide. It stretches from the Sabine River on the border with Louisiana to the Rio Grande on the border with Mexico. The total shoreline length including bays, islands, and peninsulas is about 3,300 miles. This natural region is ecologically diverse and features barrier islands, beaches, sand dunes, bays, lagoons, and estuaries with marshes, seagrass beds, and oyster reefs.

Inland on the prairie are large urban areas and busy ports, numerous oil refining and petrochemical complexes, and at one time, tallgrass prairies dominated by bluestems, Indiangrass, and paspalums that have been mostly replaced by agriculture. Many rivers and streams cross the coastal plain and provide freshwater inflow to cordgrass-dominated marshes and highly productive bays and estuaries. The river floodplains support hardwoods like oaks, elms, and pecan as well as bald cypress swamps on the northern coast.

Average annual rainfall for the prairies and marshes region varies from 56 inches in the northeast to 28 inches in the southwest and is fairly evenly distributed throughout the year. The growing season exceeds 300 days per year. Elevations range from sea level to 250 feet at the inland edge of the coastal plain. Rainfall for the Sand Plain ranges from 24 to 28 inches and elevations range from sea level to 150 feet.

The coastal plain consists of relatively young wedges of mud and sand that have been deposited into the Gulf by Texas rivers over the last 60 million years. The sediments of the coastal plain at the land surface are only a few million years old inland and the barrier islands are only 5,000 years old or younger.

Over the last few hundred thousand years, sea level has risen and fallen many times in response to the growth and melting of the great ice sheets of the last Ice Age. About 18,000 years ago, during the height of the last Ice Age, sea level was 300 to 450 feet lower than today because so much water was frozen in the great ice sheets. The Texas shoreline was then about 50 miles gulfward of the present shore. Texas rivers flowed across the exposed continental shelf sediments and cut deeply into the coastal plain. World climate warmed between 5 and 10 thousand years ago, ice sheets melted, and sea level rose reaching its present level about 5,000 years ago. As the sea level rose, the river valleys were drowned and formed the bays and estuaries of today. The Rio Grande, Colorado, and Brazos have completely filled in their bays with sediments.

Sand deposits that were submerged by the rising sea level have been pushed toward shore by waves and have helped build the barrier islands. Barrier island and beach dune sands are better stabilized by vegetation on the north coast than on the south coast. This is a result of higher rainfall in the northeast. The Coastal Sand Plain, between Riviera and Raymondville, is a windswept band of sand that has been blown inland from Padre Island (the longest barrier island in the U.S.) and the Laguna Madre (the largest hypersaline basin in the U.S.) over the last few thousand years. The dunes of the Sand Plain are mostly stabilized by tall and mid-grasses like seacoast bluestem and gulfdune paspalum mixed with live oak and mesquite. Overgrazing and fire suppression have caused woody vegetation to increase since pre-settlement times. Most of the region is owned by the King and Kenedy ranches and is grazed by cattle. The region was called the "Wild Horse Prairie" in the 1800s because of large roaming herds of free-running horses.

The beaches, bays, marshes, forests, and rivers of the coast provide numerous recreational opportunities that contribute strongly to making the coast one of the top travel destinations in Texas. The tidal saltmarshes serve as nursery areas for young shrimp, crabs, and many important fishes like flounder, redfish, and seatrout. The regional economic impact of bay- and estuary-related recreation is growing and is now about 6 times that of commercial fishing.

The Texas coast is a renowned bird-watching destination, especially for the spring "fallout" when songbirds migrating north stop to rest after crossing the Gulf. Large numbers of waterfowl from central North America spend the winter on the Texas coast and support a significant waterfowl hunting industry as well as bird-watching. A number of refuges, management areas, and preserves are operated by the U.S. Fish and Wildlife Service, National Park Service, Texas Parks and Wildlife Department, and a few private organizations such as The Nature Conservancy. These areas provide habitats for songbirds, waterfowl, and some endangered species like Attwater's prairie chicken and wintering whooping cranes. Most of these areas offer recreational opportunities and some have educational functions as well.

Saltmarsh habitat of the endangered whooping crane at the Aransas National Wildlife Refuge

Figure 9 shows the distribution of facilities in the Gulf Coast Prairies & Marshes and Coastal Sand Plain regions.

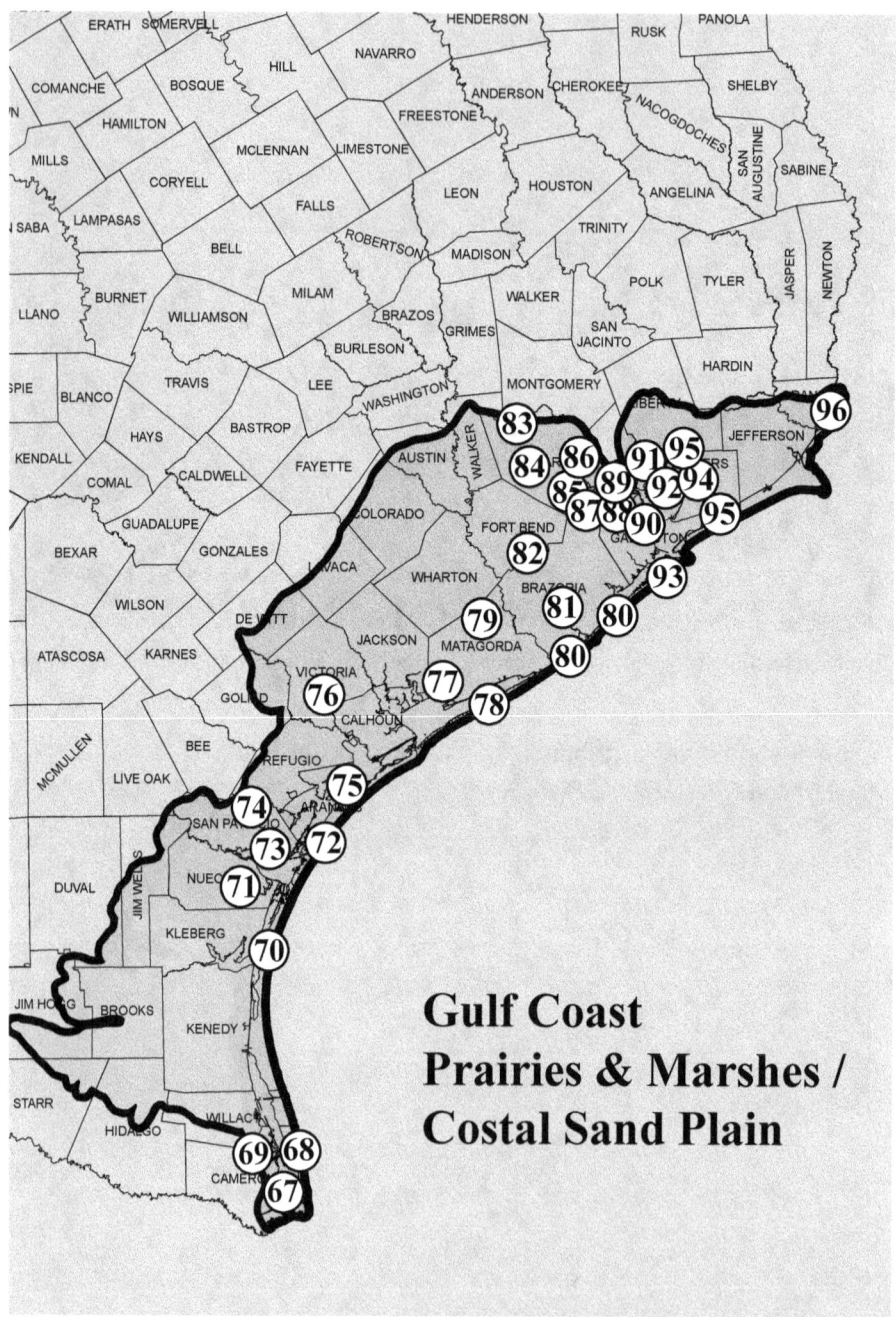

Figure 9—Facilities in the Gulf Coast Prairies & Marshes and Coastal Sand Plain regions

South Padre Island Dolphin Research & Sea Life Nature Center

110 N. Garcia, Port Isabel, TX 78578

Directors: George and Scarlet Colley

Contacts: Phone 956-299-1957; E-mail form on website

Website: http://spinaturecenter.com/

Natural Region: Gulf Coast Prairies & Marshes

Major Ecosystem(s): Gulf of Mexico; Laguna Madre

Overview: SPIDR is in Port Isabel on Lighthouse Square at the mainland end of the Queen Isabella Causeway. It emphasizes bottlenose dolphin and marine life conservation. It features aquaria with native marine animals and touch tanks with live local marine animals. The gift shop features eco-friendly souvenirs.

Fun for Kids: In addition to touch tanks with live local marine animals, marine aquaria, and exhibits, there are daily multimedia presentations about the local resident dolphins.

Family Fun: Dolphin-watching boat tours can be scheduled.

Educational: Customized school field trips can incorporate nature and beach walks. An outreach program to public and private schools, including the LRGV, features multimedia displays and hands-on living marine life exhibits. Migratory birds of the LRGV are also highlighted.

Directions: From Brownsville, take FM 1792 to Port Isabel. Turn right on Park Rd. 100 and go to Lighthouse Square at the west end of Queen Isabella Causeway. The website includes a link to a printable map.

GPS Coordinates: Latitude: 26° 04.687´ N   Longitude: 97° 12.423´ W

The South Padre Island Dolphin Research & Sea Life Nature Center

Live animal touch tanks inside SPIDR

South Padre Island Birding and Nature Center

6801 Padre Blvd., South Padre Island, TX 78597

Owner: South Padre Island B&NC   **Size:** 50 acres

Contacts: Phone 956-243-8289; Fax 956-761-4523; E-mail info@spibirding. com

Website: www.spibirding.com/

Natural Region: Gulf Coast Prairies & Marshes

Major Ecosystem(s): Gulf of Mexico; barrier island; Laguna Madre

Overview: Padre Island is one of the longest barrier islands in the world, and the Laguna Madre is one of only a few hypersaline embayments in the world. Habitats include dunes and meadows, intertidal flats, a saltmarsh, and a freshwater treatment wetland associated with the wastewater treatment plant.

SPIBNC features a main building with hands-on exhibits, an auditorium where educational films are shown, a gift shop, and a 5-story observation tower. Outside are 4,800 feet of boardwalks with 7 observation blinds and a deck overlooking the Laguna Madre. This is the only unit of the World Birding Center outside the LRGV.

Fun for Kids: Interpretive guides may be available for the hands-on exhibits in the center. There is a five-story observation tower and a nature gift shop.

Family Fun: Documentary films about local plants, animals, and ecosystems are shown in the auditorium. An online bird library is maintained on the website. Facilities can be rented for events.

Educational: The center features bird-watching and bird walks but also emphasizes conservation and environmental awareness. Volunteer guides give tours of the boardwalks and discuss the local habitats. Guided tours for school and other groups can be scheduled.

Directions: In South Padre Island, go 4.5 miles north of Queen Isabella Causeway on Park Rd. 100 (Padre Blvd.) to SPIBNC on the left, just south of the Convention Center. The website includes a printable map.

GPS Coordinates: Latitude: 26°08.240′N   Longitude: 97°10.428′W

The South Padre Island Birding & Nature Center

Boardwalks in the Laguna Madre wetlands at SPIBNC

Laguna Atascosa National Wildlife Refuge

22817 Ocelot Rd., Los Fresnos, TX 78566

Owner: U.S. Fish & Wildlife Service **Size:** 45,187 acres (main unit); 97,000 acres total

Contacts: Phone 956-748-3607; Fax 956-748-3609; E-mail FW2_RW_ Laguna@fws.gov

Website: http://www.friendsofsouthtexasrefuges.org/?id=224

Natural Region: Gulf Coast Prairies & Marshes

Major Ecosystem(s): Laguna Madre; coastal wetlands, prairie, thorn forest

Overview: The refuge impounds freshwater in ponds, resacas, and the central Laguna Atascosa ("muddy lake" in Spanish). These support freshwater wetlands and riparian vegetation. Other habitats include wind tidal flats, coastal prairie, thorn scrub forest, and seagrass beds in the Laguna Madre. The refuge has high biodiversity, including more bird species than any other refuge in the U.S.

The refuge has a VC with Nature Store, 7 nature trails, and 2 self-guided auto tour roads. Biking is allowed on tour roads and designated trails.

Fun for Kids: The VC features exhibits and videos. Volunteers and rangers lead a variety of year-round programs including guided nature walks, birding tours, and van tours.

Family Fun: The Friends of Laguna Atascosa NWR offer guided tours, including an open-air tram tour (October–March). The Friends also offer guided kayak tours on the Laguna Madre (summer only). There is an annual Ocelot Conservation Festival.

Educational: Schools and other groups may call to arrange for programs. School groups enter free (including teachers, aides, and parents). Free school outreach programs that emphasize native and endangered wildlife of South Texas are offered. They also provide teacher resources geared to incorporating environmental education into curricula, as well as Project WILD and other educator workshops.

Directions: From Harlingen, go east on FM 106 18 miles past Rio Hondo. Go left at the T (Buena Vista Rd.) and continue 3 miles to the VC. The website includes a printable map.

GPS Coordinates: Latitude: 26° 13.755'N   Longitude: 97° 20.835'W

The Laguna Atascosa National Wildlife Refuge VC

Wildlife exhibits in the VC at Laguna Atascosa NWR

70 Padre Island National Seashore

20402 Park Rd. 22, Corpus Christi, TX 78418

Owner: U.S. National Park Service   **Size:** 130,434 acres

Contacts: Phone 361-949-8068; Fax 361-949-9951; E-mail form on website

Website: www.nps.gov/pais/index.htm

Natural Region: Gulf Coast Prairies & Marshes

Major Ecosystem(s): Gulf of Mexico; barrier island; Laguna Madre

Overview: This barrier island is named for Padre Nicolas Balli, a Spanish missionary who established the first permanent settlement on the island. PINS protects the longest remaining undeveloped stretch of barrier island in the world. Between the island and the mainland is the Laguna Madre ("mother lake" in Spanish), one of only 6 hypersaline lagoons in the world. The island includes beaches on the Gulf shore, dunes, grasslands and marshes, and extensive wind-tidal mudflats on the Laguna shore. This is the most important nesting beach in the U.S. for the Kemp's ridley, which is currently the world's most endangered sea turtle. About 380 species of birds have been documented in the park because of its location in the Central Flyway migration route.

Fun for Kids: The Junior Ranger program is for ages 5–13. The WebRangers online program (www.webrangers.us) is for all ages. The online magazine *The Gulf Breeze* is available on the website.

Family Fun: Rangers guide beach walks and give deck talks daily on the natural and cultural history of the island. Hatchling sea turtle release events are held.

Educational: The Environmental Education (EE) division offers free classes and programs to K–12 school classes that are aligned with state education standards. Rangers conduct programs at the park or at schools/institutions, and lessons can be modified to meet group needs. Most programs deal with sea turtles or other wildlife and fishes, or problems such as beach trash. Some programs deal with cultural history. Entry is free for groups participating in park-led environmental education programs. The Malaquite VC has a bookstore where teachers get a 20 percent discount.

Directions: From Corpus Christi, take South Padre Island Dr. (TX 358) east and cross the JFK Causeway (Park Rd. 22). Go 10 miles south on PR 22 to the entrance. The website includes a printable map.

GPS Coordinates: Latitude: 27° 28.465ʹN   Longitude: 97° 17.078ʹW

The Padre Island National Seashore VC at Malaquite Pavilion

Sea turtle models inside the VC at Padre Island NS

Boardwalks over the fragile beach dunes at Padre Island NS

South Texas Botanical Gardens & Nature Center

8545 S. Staples St., Corpus Christi, TX 78413

Owner: Botanical & Nature Institute of South Texas, Inc.   **Size:** 182 acres

Contacts: Phone 361-852-2100; Fax 361-852-7875; E-mail wmwomack@ stxbot.org

Website: http://stxbot.org/

Natural Region: Gulf Coast Prairies & Marshes

Major Ecosystem(s): Oso Creek riparian; impounded fresh marsh

Overview: The site is on Oso Creek. It emphasizes various gardens and floral exhibits but also includes some native habitats. The Oso Creek Loop Trail runs along the riparian vegetation of the creek. The impounded wetland, Gator Lake, includes a Wetlands Awareness Boardwalk, Palapa Grande overlook, and bird observation tower. There is a seasonal butterfly garden and walk-through butterfly house, as well as a reptile and amphibian exhibit.

There is no charge to enter the VC and Nature's Boutique.

Fun for Kids: Wilderness Experience Summer Nature Studies is summer day camp for kids ages 5–9 in June and July. There are live reptile and amphibian exhibits.

Family Fun: Special events include the annual Big Bloom plant sale in April. There is a seasonal walk-through butterfly house and garden.

Educational: Adult and school/youth group self-guided and docent-guided tours can be scheduled. Education classes and workshops for adults emphasize South Texas plants and various conservation topics. The Winter Lecture Series (Jan.–Feb.) on Wednesday mornings deals with a variety of nature and horticultural topics.

Directions: From South Padre Island Dr. (TX 358) in Corpus Christi, take S. Staples exit and turn south. Follow the green direction signs on Staples (FM 2444) and cross the bridge over Oso Creek. The entrance is on the right immediately after the curve. The website includes a printable map.

GPS Coordinates: Latitude: 27°39.157'N   Longitude: 97°24.434'W

The VC at South Texas Botanical Gardens & Nature Center

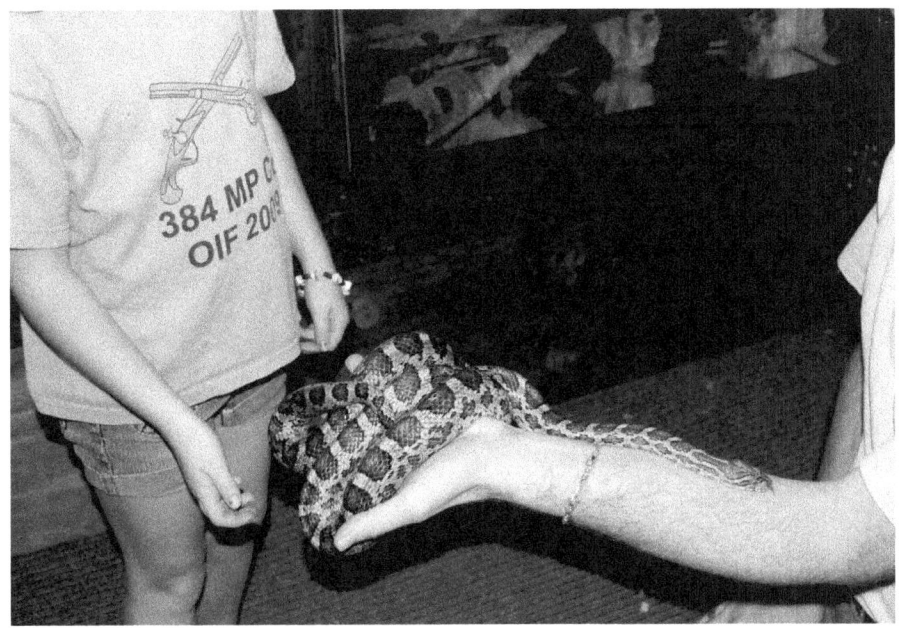

Live snakes on exhibit in the VC at STBG&NC

Inside the butterfly house and garden at STBG&NC

72 University of Texas Marine Science Institute

630 E. Cotter Ave., Port Aransas, TX 78373

Owner: Univ. of Texas at Austin   **Size:** 3.5 acres (Wetlands Education Center)

Contacts: Phone 361-749-6729; Fax 361-749-6777; E-mail mailto:sara.pelleteri@mail.utexas.edu

Website: www.utmsi.utexas.edu

Natural Region: Gulf Coast Prairies & Marshes

Major Ecosystem(s): Gulf of Mexico; Aransas/Corpus Christi Bay estuaries

Overview: UTMSI is on the Aransas Pass ship channel. A major mission of MSI is to educate the public about the importance of the world's oceans and coasts. It promotes interest in marine science through educational programs for teachers, students, and the general public.

Facilities include a VC with 7 aquaria featuring Texas coastal habitats and organisms and other displays. The Ocean Emporium features educational items and souvenirs. The 3.5 acre Wetlands Education Center features a constructed tidal marsh and seagrass pond with boardwalks.

Fun for Kids: Free summer Birding 101 classes are for kids ages 7–16. The VC offers self-guided tours and educational films.

Family Fun: Wetlands Education Family Science Night uses state-aligned activities to teach wetland values. The Road Scholar (formerly Elderhostel) program offers travel/adventure to active seniors.

Educational: Tours for school groups can be arranged in advance. The Wetlands Education Center also offers guided tours that educate schoolchildren and visitors about the importance and values of wetlands. Visiting school groups can sail on the Research Vessel *KATY* to learn about marine environments through sampling and measurement. Teacher workshops use marine science topics and techniques to develop state-aligned lessons in all subjects.

Directions: From the Port Aransas ferry, go straight on Cotter Ave. through both stop lights and the 4-way stop sign toward the beach. UTMSI is on the left before you get to the beach. The website includes a printable map.

GPS Coordinates: Latitude: 27° 50.123´ N   Longitude: 97° 03.097´ W

The University of Texas Marine Science Institute VC

A Wetlands Education Center boardwalk tour at UTMSI

73 Texas State Aquarium

2710 N Shoreline Blvd., Corpus Christi, TX 78402

Owner: Texas State Aquarium   **Size:** over 7 acres

Contacts: Phone 361-881-1200 or 1-800-477-GULF; Fax 361-881-1257; E-mail mermaid@txstateaq.org

Website: www.texasstateaquarium.org

Natural Region: Gulf Coast Prairies & Marshes

Major Ecosystems: Marine aquaria, touch pools, and outdoor saltmarsh; Corpus Christi Bay and Rincon Channel

Overview: Indoor exhibits include an Amazon rainforest in addition to large aquaria featuring marine organisms such as jellyfishes, fishes, and habitats such as a coral reef and an oil drilling platform. There are touch pools and interactive computer kiosks that teach about habitats of the Laguna Madre and Padre Island bays and estuaries. Outside are exhibits featuring dolphins, birds of prey, river otters, stingrays, alligators, sea turtles, and a saltmarsh with boardwalk. There is also a zero-depth water play area and an interactive fossil dig site.

The SeaLab Education Center is on Rincon Channel 1.5 miles from TSA.

Fun for Kids: Camp-in programs are sleepovers (for ages 7–18) that include dinner and breakfast. Topics include tours, games, oceanography, and scouting programs. SeaCamp offers summer day camps for ages pre-K–9 that cover a variety of ecological and environmental outdoor activities. Scholarships based on financial need may be available.

Coastal Outdoors Adventure School of Texas 2-day science adventures are for ages 9–13.

Family Fun: Sensational Sustainable Seafood cooking classes are held the second Tuesday monthly.

Educational: Field trips to TSA can be self-guided tours (pre-K–12) or staff-guided (grades 3–12). Programs include indoor tours and some programs visit the shoreline outside or a local wetland to observe birds. All tours include teacher resources, and a field trip packet is available online. SeaLab programs are staff-guided and include teacher resources. Topics include fish anatomy, human impacts on habitats and ecosystems, resource management, marine biology, and a wetlands canoe trip. The school outreach programs bring interactive and live animal opportunities to the schoolroom. Homeschool classes for grades K–secondary are offered several times a year. The Aquavision distance learning program for K–12 is aligned with state education standards and covers a wide array of marine ecology and environmental topics.

Professional development courses for CPE credit include Projects WILD and WILD Aquatic, Growing Up WILD, etc.

Directions: From Corpus Christi, take Hwy 181N-Harbor Bridge exit. Cross the bridge and take the first exit (Corpus Christi Beach). Follow the curve and turn right on Burleson St. Go to the first stop sign and turn right onto Surfside. Continue to the TSA sign and parking lots.

GPS Coordinates: Latitude: 27° 48.891' N   Longitude: 97° 23.528' W

The Texas State Aquarium waterfall entrance

The Texas State Aquarium has lots of live marine animals

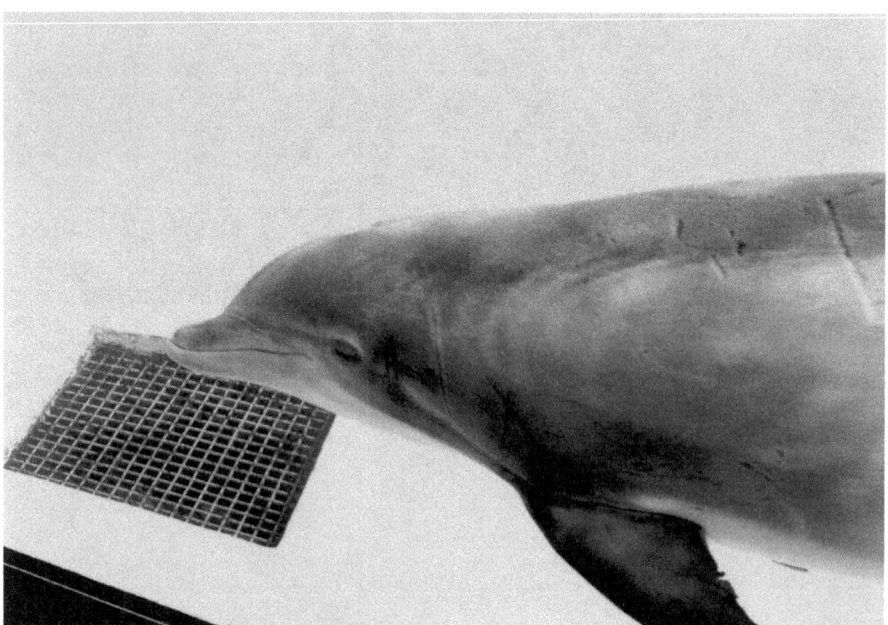

The Texas State Aquarium has a live dolphin show

Welder Wildlife Refuge

10620 US Hwy 77, Sinton, TX 78387

Owner: Rob & Bessie Welder Wildlife Foundation   **Size:** 7,800 acres

Contacts: Phone 361-364-2643; Fax 361-364-2650; E-mail website forms

Website: www.welderwildlife.org

Natural Region: Gulf Coast Prairies & Marshes

Major Ecosystem(s): Aransas River riparian hardwood corridor; prairie grasslands/ponds/wetlands

Overview: The Aransas River borders the refuge and supports hardwood riparian corridors. Lakes and ponds support fringing marshes. Grasslands are managed jointly for wildlife and livestock. These habitats provide an outdoor classroom and laboratory. A varied array of public tours, school and college programs, teacher in-service programs, conservation workshops, symposia, and field days are led by professional staff year-round.

Fun for Kids: Special programs and tours designed for individual groups can be scheduled for groups of 10 or more. Welder is a working ranch as well as a wildlife management area.

Family Fun: There are free public tours every Thursday afternoon and some Saturdays. There are free conservation workshops/field days for landowners.

Educational: The Conservation Education Program serves public school and university groups and emphasizes ecology and management of South Texas wildlife and their habitats. Education programs are designed for students from K–12 and through college. Programs consist of 0.5 to 2 days of field activities on South Texas ecology, and can be adapted to individual groups. School programs/tours are free of charge. For programs longer than a day, groups have the option of staying overnight at the refuge for a modest charge. Staff members work with classroom teachers and visit classrooms to assist with program activities. Programs assist teachers with meeting state education requirements. Teacher and adult education programs, workshops, and field days include a wide range of conservation and ecology topics. Some teacher programs offer CPE credits.

Directions: From Sinton, go about 7 miles north on US Hwy 77. Look for the brown sign on the right. The website includes printable directions and a map.

GPS Coordinates: Latitude: 28° 07.279´ N   Longitude: 97° 26.522´ W

The Welder Wildlife Refuge headquarters

One of the extensive collections at the Welder Wildlife Refuge museum

Aransas National Wildlife Refuge Complex

1 Wildlife Circle, Austwell, TX 77950

Owner: U.S. Fish & Wildlife Service   **Size:** 115,000 acres

Contacts: Phone 361-286-3559; Fax 361-286-3722;
E-mail mailto:felipe_prieto@fws.gov

Website: www.fws.gov/refuge/aransas/

Natural Region: Gulf Coast Prairies & Marshes

Major Ecosystem(s): San Antonio Bay; fresh/tidal marshes, prairie, woodlands

Overview: Located on the Blackjack Peninsula in the Coastal Bend region, ANWR is world famous as the wintering area for the endangered whooping crane. It harbors many other species in various habitats including coastal brush, woodlands, and prairie, as well as fresh and tidal wetlands and a large barrier island (Matagorda Island).

Facilities include a VC with interpretive displays/exhibits/programs and a bookstore, a 16-mile self-guided auto tour loop, a 40-foot observation tower overlooking San Antonio Bay, boardwalk and viewing decks, 7 walking trails, a picnic area with restrooms, a Youth Environmental Training Area, and an Environmental Education Center on Matagorda Island.

Fun for Kids: There is a live alligator viewing area near the VC and a 40-foot observation tower overlooking San Antonio Bay.

Family Fun: There is year-round kayak/canoe access to San Antonio Bay and a 16-mile self-guided auto tour loop.

Educational: The refuge has an Environmental Education (EE) specialist on staff. Resources for teachers, students, groups, and the public are varied. These include on-site presentations, outreach programs for schools/groups, winter van tours (sponsored by Friends of Aransas and Matagorda Island), and a variety of wildlife, ecology, and environmental classes aligned with state education standards. A variety of printed resources are available as well as books at the VC store. The Youth Environmental Training Area is available for groups participating in the Environmental Education program. The Matagorda Island EE Center offers classes in beach, bay, and marsh ecology.

Group service projects are available upon request.

Directions: From US Hwy 77, take either TX 239 (south of Victoria) or FM 774 in Refugio to Austwell. One mile south of Austwell take FM 2040 for 7 miles to the refuge. The website includes a printable map.

GPS Coordinates: Latitude: 28° 18.633´N   Longitude: 96° 48.091´W

The Aransas National Wildlife Refuge VC

A large wetland observation tower at Aransas NWR

An alligator viewing area at Aransas NWR

76 INVISTA Victoria ISD Wetlands

Victoria Independent School District

John Snyder-Wetland Science Educator

102 Prospect Dr., P.O. Box 1759, Victoria, TX 77902

Owner: INVISTA   **Size:** 55 acres

Contacts: Phone 361-572-1153; Fax 361-572-1118;
E-mail Wetlandspecialist@gmail.com

Website: www.visd.com/links/invista/index.asp

Natural Region: Gulf Coast Prairies & Marshes

Major Ecosystem(s): constructed freshwater treatment wetlands

Overview: The wetland education area is a collaborative program of the VISD and the INVISTA Victoria manufacturing facility. Constructed in 1996, the wetland provides secondary polishing for the site's wastewater stream that has been treated in an above-ground biological treatment facility before entering the wetland. Water quality meets Texas water discharge standards as it exits the biological treatment facility and enters the wetland. The water is returned to the Guadalupe River after passing through the wetland.

The INVISTA Wetland Education Center, in the heart of the wetland, is a state-of-the-art outdoor science lab with microscopes and other wetland science equipment to support fourth grade through college level science curricula. The program has a full-time resident wetland environmental science educator. The wetlands have been certified by the National Wildlife Habitat Council "Corporate Lands for Learning" program.

The INVISTA Wetland and associated education program is not open to the general public and available to schools by appointment only. Directions are provided when a field trip is scheduled.

Educational: The education program is called the Wetland Environmental Science Education Encounter (WE SEE). The curriculum is aligned with state education standards for science for grades 4–12. Topics include soil, water chemistry, plants, animals, microbiology, and application of the scientific method. The curriculum aids teachers in meeting the state student hands-on requirement.

School groups from as far as 275 miles away have utilized this program. There is a nominal charge for schools from outside VISD.

Directions: Detailed directions are provided when a school field trip is scheduled.

The INVISTA Wetlands wet lab/instruction area

The INVISTA Wetlands constructed treatment wetlands

Texas State Marine Education Center

102 Marine Center Dr., Palacios, TX 77465

Owner: Palacios ISD/Matagorda County Navigation Dist. #1   **Size:** 60 acres

Contacts: Phone 361-972-3774; Fax 361-972-1174; E-mail tsmeck12@tisd.net

Website: http://www.palaciosisd.org/vnews/display.v/SEC/
Texas%20State%20Marine%20Education%20Center

Natural Region: Gulf Coast Prairies & Marshes

Major Ecosystem(s): Tres Palacios Bay; estuarine saltmarsh/flats; coastal prairie

Overview: Tres Palacios Bay in Matagorda County is an inlet of Matagorda Bay. TSMEC includes 2,400 feet of bay frontage with a beach, over 80 acres of saltmarsh, and some coastal prairie. Facilities include a classroom building, a pier, a 1.25 mile nature trail with observation platform, and two 12-passenger teaching vessels.

This facility is not a drop-by type program. Schools outside the Palacios ISD may use the program for a nominal fee.

Family Fun: There is public access to the Karankawa Trace Nature Trail.

Educational: This program offers lessons for pre-K–12 level students and teachers through hands-on marine oriented activities in the field and lab. The curriculum is aligned with state education standards. Over 100 lessons emphasize erosion, plants, birds, sea life, water quality/pollution, history, and other topics.

A standard marine science field trip would include study of Matagorda Bay water quality and marine organisms by boat, seining and identification of marsh and estuarine organisms, study of fish characteristics and fish printing, and study of plants and animals along the Karankawa Trace Nature Trail.

Professional development opportunities for teachers are also offered.

Directions: In Palacios, from the intersection of Business 35 and Margerum Rd., go west on B-35 0.6 mile to Camp Hulen Rd. Turn left (south) on Camp Hulen Rd. and go 0.7 mile to entrance. The website includes a link to a map and driving directions.

GPS Coordinates: Latitude: 28° 41.705´N   Longitude: 96° 14.415´ W

The Texas State Marine Education Center

The Karankawa Trace Nature Trail marsh boardwalk at TSMEC

Matagorda Bay Nature Park

6430 FM 2031, Matagorda, TX 77457

Owner: Lower Colorado River Authority   **Size:** 1,600 acres

Contacts: Phone 1-800-776-5272 x4740; E-mail form on website

Website: www.lcra.org/parks/developed_parks/matagorda.html

Natural Region: Gulf Coast Prairies & Marshes

Major Ecosystem(s): Gulf of Mexico; East Matagorda Bay/Colorado River estuary

Overview: MBNP is on the Matagorda Peninsula at the mouth of the Colorado River. It features 2 miles of Gulf beach and 2 miles of river frontage plus hundreds of acres of saltmarshes and beach dunes.

Facilities include a Natural Science Center with classrooms and exhibits, trails with shaded wildlife viewing areas, a group pavilion and covered picnic shelters, fishing piers on the river and Gulf, and a small store and kayak rental facility. RV and tent camping are available. Facilities meet ADA requirements and can be rented for private events.

Fun for Kids: There are scouting and youth group programs, including some merit badge programs, which can be customized to your group's needs.

Family Fun: Community programs, usually scheduled on Saturdays, include bay and river kayaking trips, beachcombing, wetland birding, nature scavenger hunts, etc.

Educational: A wide variety of educational programs features Gulf of Mexico and estuarine ecology, water quality/watershed management, water conservation, beach and dune processes, use of GPS units, etc. All programs are grade-level appropriate and aligned with state education standards. Most programs can be tailored to meet the needs of your class, youth group, or organization.

Directions: From Bay City in Matagorda County, go south about 20 miles on TX 60 to Matagorda. Turn left (south) on FM 2031 and follow the Colorado River about 6.5 miles to the Gulf. The website includes a link to a printable map and directions.

GPS Coordinates: Latitude: 28°35.915´N   Longitude: 95°58.703´W

The Matagorda Bay Nature Park Natural Science Center

Matagorda County Birding Nature Center

1025 State Hwy 35 S, Bay City, TX 77414

Owner: Matagorda County Nature Center, Inc.   **Size:** 34 acres

Contacts: Phone 979-245-3336; E-mail mcbnc@mcbnc.org

Website: www.mcbnc.org

Natural Region: Gulf Coast Prairies & Marshes

Major Ecosystem(s): Colorado River floodplain

Overview: MCBNC is on the Colorado River just less than 2 miles west of Bay City on SH 35. Natural habitats include the river, a small tributary stream, riparian and upland hardwood forest, and a wildflower field (prairie). There are impounded ponds, a wetland with a boardwalk, a waterfall, and stream crossings. There are 6 specialized gardens.

Other features include three trails, entry kiosk and learning center, an outdoor education center, astronomy pad, a pier on the river, and a bird/photo blind on the wetland. Golf carts can be rented by the mobility impaired.

Fun for Kids: Paddling on the Colorado River is available.

Family Fun: There are hummingbird and butterfly gardens in season.

Educational: Education programs are offered to school, family, and civic groups. The curriculum includes 3 classes for grades pre-K–2 and 5 classes for grades 3–8. Classes are aligned with state education standards and feature subjects such as ponds, ecology, gardening, birds, mammals, trees, and insects and spiders. Teachers may borrow education trunks to take to their classrooms. Self-guided tours are also allowed.

MCBNC hosts 4-H, Master Naturalist, and Master Gardener training courses. Occasional teacher workshops are held. Speakers for nature seminars can be scheduled.

Directions: From Bay City, go west just under 2 miles on SH 35. The entrance is on the left just before the LCRA canal. The website includes a printable map.

GPS Coordinates: Latitude: 28° 59.060˙N   Longitude: 96° 00.780˙ W

The Matagorda County Birding Nature Center entrance

The outdoor education center at MCBNC

The dock and deck on the Colorado River at MCBNC

Texas Mid-Coast National Wildlife Refuge Complex

2547 CR 316, Brazoria, TX 77422

Owner: U.S. Fish & Wildlife Service   **Size:** about 100,000 acres (3 refuges)

Contacts: Phone 979-964-4011; Fax 979-964-4021;
E-mail mailto:tom_schneider@fws.gov

Website: http://www.fws.gov/southwest/refuges/texas/texasmidcoast/index.htm

Natural Region: Gulf Coast Prairies & Marshes

Major Ecosystem(s): coastal bays, wetlands, prairies; bottomland forest

Overview: The Mid-coast Refuge Complex consists of Brazoria, San Bernard, and Big Boggy National Wildlife Refuges. These units include many coastal habitats such as bay shores, tidal and freshwater wetlands and streams, coastal prairie, and bottomland hardwood forests. These refuges are famous bird-watching destinations. In the spring, birds migrating north seem to fall out of the sky to rest and feed after crossing the Gulf of Mexico. Wintering waterfowl are seen in spectacular numbers. They also provide excellent study areas for coastal wetland ecology.

Fun for Kids: There are interpretive exhibits at the Discovery Center at Brazoria NWR.

Family Fun: San Bernard NWR has a 7-mile auto tour route and 5 trails including 1 to the champion live oak in Texas. Brazoria NWR also has a 9-mile auto-tour route and 1.5 miles of trails. The Dow Woods Unit in Lake Jackson has 2.5 miles of handicapped-accessible trails.

Educational: The refuge, along with volunteers and partners, sponsors the Discovery Environmental Education Program (DEEP). This program provides hands-on experience where students at all levels and ages can discover the natural world. The program is headquartered at the Discovery Center at Brazoria NWR. Activities include seining a saltmarsh, dip-netting a freshwater pond, and learning about water chemistry and the importance of wetlands to fisheries.

The Discover Outpost at the Hudson Woods Unit of San Bernard NWR emphasizes the ecology of a bottomland forest and the environmental impact of invasive species. Field trips should be scheduled at least 3 weeks in advance (979-964-4011).

Directions to Brazoria NWR: From the intersection of Hwy 288 and FM 523 in Angleton, take FM 523 to the Hwy 2004 intersection. Go 5.5 miles on FM 523 to CR 227. Turn left on CR 227 and go just under 2 miles to the refuge entrance. The Discovery Center is 3 miles east of the entrance. The website includes printable maps.

GPS Coordinates: Latitude: 29° 03.908′ N   Longitude: 95° 19.153′ W

Directions to San Bernard NWR: From the intersection of Hwy 288 and FM 2004, turn right on 2004. Go 14 miles to FM 2918. Turn left and go 1 mile. Turn right on CR 306. Go 2 miles to tour road entrance on the left.

GPS Coordinates: Latitude: 28° 54.424′ N   Longitude: 95° 35.478′ W

The Brazoria National Wildlife Refuge Discovery Center

The wetland boardwalk at the Discovery Center at Brazoria NWR

A wild alligator seen from the boardwalk at Brazoria NWR

Sea Center Texas

300 Medical Dr., Lake Jackson, TX 77566

Owner: Texas Parks & Wildlife Dept.   **Size:** 75 acres

Contacts: Phone 979-292-0100; Fax 979-292-0566; E-mail seacenter@tpwd.texas.gov

Website: www.tpwd.state.tx.us/spdest/visitorcenters/seacenter/

Natural Region: Gulf Coast Prairies & Marshes

Major Ecosystem(s): constructed salt and freshwater marshes; redfish hatchery

Overview: Sea Center Texas is the largest redfish hatchery in the world with 36 one-acre fish culture ponds. Education about marine fish and their habitat needs is also a primary mission. The VC features seven different marine aquaria, a touch tank, and exhibits of Texas marine life.

Outside, a 600-foot boardwalk accesses a constructed 1-acre saltmarsh and a 3-acre fresh marsh. The wetland area is part of the Great Texas Coastal Birding Trail and also features a Wildscape Demonstration Garden. There is also a Youth Fishing Pond.

Admission is free. Facilities are ADA-accessible.

Fun for Kids: Youth fishing events are offered periodically or by reservation at the Youth Fishing Pond.

Family Fun: Special events such as Nature Day and National Fishing Day are held periodically. Guided tours of the VC, wetlands, and hatchery can be arranged.

Educational: SCT offers a variety of free educational programs and events. Tours of the wetlands, VC, and fish hatchery can be arranged. Self-guided VC tours are available. Lessons on water quality and fish adaptations are offered. A variety of teacher resources including wetland education trunks are available.

Directions: In Lake Jackson, take SH 288 south to Plantation Dr. Go west on Plantation Dr. for 0.75 mile to the intersection of Medical Dr. Go right on Medical Dr. and about 0.1 mile to SCT. The website includes a printable map.

GPS Coordinates: Latitude: 29° 01.105' N   Longitude: 95° 26.735' W

The Sea Center Texas VC

The Sea Center Texas kids fishing pond

Kids of all ages enjoy the aquariums at Sea Center Texas

A live animal touch tank at Sea Center Texas

Brazos Bend State Park

21901 FM 762, Needville, TX 77461

Owner: Texas Parks & Wildlife Dept.   **Size:** about 5,000 acres

Contacts: Phone 979-553-5101; E-mail David.Heinicke@tpwd.state.tx.us

Website: www.brazosbend.org

Natural Region: Gulf Coast Prairies & Marshes

Major Ecosystem(s): Brazos River floodplain forests and wetlands; coastal prairie

Overview: BBSP, about 40 miles southwest of downtown Houston, has over 3 miles of frontage on the Brazos River. Big Creek crosses the park and has adjacent sloughs and oxbow lakes. These support alligators and other reptiles, amphibians, and mammals. The river and creek support bottomland hardwood forests. There are some remnant areas of upland coastal prairie. These support wildflowers and butterflies seasonally. These habitats provide excellent birding (over 300 species recorded) and alligator watching.

There are 35 miles of hike/bike trails, including 8 miles of equestrian trails and a short nature/interpretive trail. Facilities include platforms for wildlife viewing and an observation tower.

Fun for Kids: The Eco-Explorers Summer Program Series for Children meets 1 day a week throughout June and July. A wide variety of nature-related topics are covered for kids ages 3–14.

Family Fun: The George Observatory, a satellite of the Houston Museum of Natural Science, is open Saturdays and offers programs on astronomy. The Creekfield Lake Nature Trail is paved and ADA accessible and has interpretive panels and an accessible boardwalk and observation deck, rest areas, and shaded benches. There are at least 6 free nature-related programs and hikes every weekend.

Educational: The Nature Center features a "Habitats and Niches" display with hands-on alligator discovery area, a tactile model of the park, freshwater aquarium, live native snakes, a touch table, and an orientation video. Interpretive staff and volunteers offer weekday guided hikes and programs for schools and other groups.

Directions: BBSP is about a 1-hour drive from Houston. Take Hwy 59 south to Crabb River Rd. exit. You can also take SH 288 south to FM 1462 West. Follow FM 1462 to FM 762 North. From the south, take SH 288 north to the FM 1462 exit or take SH 36 to FM 1462 East. All routes are marked with brown signs to guide you. The website includes a map.

GPS Coordinates: Latitude: 29° 22.285´N   Longitude: 95° 38.447´W

The Brazos Bend State Park Nature Center

The George Observatory at Brazos Bend State Park

Exhibits inside the Nature Center at Brazos Bend State Park

83 Kleb Woods Nature Center

20303 Draper Rd., Tomball, TX 77377

Owner: Harris County Precinct 3   **Size:** 133.5 acres

Contacts: Phone 281-357-5324; E-mail klebwoods@hctx.net

Website: www.pct3.hctx.net/parks/klebwoodsnaturepres.aspx

Natural Region: Gulf Coast Prairies & Marshes

Major Ecosystem(s): former tallgrass prairie/farmland now forested (mixed pine-hardwood)

Overview: Kleb Woods Nature Preserve was originally tallgrass prairie that was farmed by early German immigrants. The last owner, Elmer Kleb, allowed the farm to return to nature and actively planted trees to attract wildlife. It is now a mixed pine-hardwood forest with trees such as loblolly pine, eastern red cedar, live oak, and other hardwoods. The site includes 6 natural wetland areas and a small remnant prairie. In addition to the nature center, which has an auditorium and a classroom, the site includes the historic Kleb farm buildings. There are over 1.5 miles of trails, including wetland trails with boardwalks. The nature center has an interpretive nature trail.

The northern portion of the preserve features 10 overnight campsites for supervised scout groups only (281-496-2177 for reservations). There are also picnic sites including two that are handicapped-accessible. All programs are free to the public.

Fun for Kids: Eagle Scout and troop service projects and badge workshops are available. Other volunteer opportunities are also available.

Family Fun: The Hummingbird Festival is the third Saturday in September. Tours of the historic Kleb Farm are given on request. The Spring Bird Migration Celebration has live birds, education programs, and kids' activities. Monthly events like fourth Saturday Blue Grass Music, and second Saturday Ask the Naturalist are offered. .

Educational: The nature center and historic farm are open daily. Classes are open to individuals; most classes are attended by homeschooled kids and seniors ("K to gray"). Special programs are offered for school groups and other organizations. The facilities will support groups up to 120 students/adults. Programs include weekly Wednesday bird walks, bird study and banding classes, journaling, wildlife, vegetable and heritage gardening, native plant study, Chinese tallow control, and research projects.

Folklore and cultural heritage related programs, including weekly German language classes, are offered.

Directions: From northwest Houston, take the Northwest Freeway (US 290/ SH 6) to the Mueschke Rd. exit just west of Cypress. Go about 7 miles north on Mueschke Rd. to Draper Rd. Turn left on Draper and go about 0.2 mile to the parking lot. The website includes a link to a printable map.

GPS Coordinates: Latitude: 30° 04.345' N   Longitude: 95° 44.405' W

The Kleb Woods Nature Center VC

The historic Kleb family farm at Kleb Woods Nature Center

84 Bayou Land Conservancy

Little Cypress Creek Preserve, 14900 Telge Rd., Cypress, TX 77429

Owner: Harris County Precinct 4 Parks Dept.   **Size:** 58 acres

Conservation easement holder: Bayou Land Conservancy

Contacts: Phone 281-576-1634; E-mail info@bayouland.org

Website: www.bayoulandconservancy.org

Natural Region: Gulf Coast Prairies & Marshes

Major Ecosystems: Little Cypress Creek; floodplain forest, ponds, and wetlands

Overview: BLC is a land preservation organization that works with willing landowners to protect land in the greater Houston region. This includes river and bayou corridors and other land with significant wildlife habitat and recreational values.

BLC is included in this book because of their "No Child Left Inside" environmental education program. The objective is to get children outside to enjoy local natural areas and learn about local ecosystems. The program connects tomorrow's conservation leaders with nature today. Program field trips take place at Little Cypress Creek Preserve near Cypress in northwest Harris County. The preserve has frontage on Little Cypress Creek and habitats that include floodplain forest with river birch, flowering dogwood, red maple, black walnut, shortleaf pine, and carnivorous sundew and bladderwort plants.

Fun for Kids: A scout forestry badge program is offered.

Family Fun: The preserve is open free to the public on weekends. There are special events like BioBlitz for Beginners to document plant and animal species.

Educational: The environmental education program features science education field trips for grades 5–12. Field activities focus on wetland and water quality issues, study of invasive plant species, and native plants and animals. The connection between the health of local watersheds and the health of the Galveston Bay and Gulf of Mexico ecosystems is stressed. Programs are aligned with state education standards and include a pre-quiz and post-quiz to assess what students have learned about water and local ecology issues. There is no fee for this program. The only expense for the school is transportation. Title 1 schools may be eligible for a transportation cost waiver. Occasional teacher workshops for CPE credit are offered. Service learning projects and volunteer opportunities are available.

Directions: From US 290 west of Houston, exit onto Telge Rd. and go north for about 4 miles. Continue through the first intersection with Spring Cypress Rd. and cross over Little Cypress Creek. Go to the light at the second intersection with Spring Cypress Rd. and turn left into the preserve.

GPS Coordinates: Latitude: 29° 59.461˙ N   Longitude: 95° 39.206˙ W

The Little Cypress Creek Preserve

Edith L. Moore Nature Sanctuary

440 Wilchester Blvd., Houston, TX 77079

Owner: Houston Audubon Society   **Size:** 17.5 acres

Contacts: Phone 713-932-1639; Fax 713-461-2911; E-mail info@houstonaudubon.org

Website: http://www.houstonaudubon.org/default.aspx/MenuItemID/883/MenuGroup/Sanctuaries2.htm

Natural Region: Gulf Coast Prairies & Marshes

Major Ecosystem(s): Rummel Creek floodplain forests and ponds

Overview: ELMNS is in west Houston on Rummel Creek, a tributary of Buffalo Bayou. It houses Houston Audubon's administrative offices as well as the docent education and outreach programs, which are housed in the restored Edith L. Moore log cabin.

Trails through mixed pine-hardwood forests and around ponds provide hands-on exploration such as pond dip-netting and the live education animals. Reservations are required for all visiting groups. The site is open to the public from dawn until dusk every day.

Fun for Kids: Summer day camps for ages 2½–12 are offered June through August. The Titmouse Club is for preschoolers and includes stories, nature walks, crafts, etc. Themes focus on Houston-area animals and habitats. The After-School Nature Explorers Club is a monthly program for school kids that focuses on local ecology topics.

Family Fun: Owl Prowls are offered November–February.

Educational: The docents provide guided natural history field trips for schools, scout troops, and any interested group. Field trips use the wooded trails and freshwater ponds of the sanctuary, and can be customized to curriculum or scout achievement needs.

The outreach program to local schools and libraries uses hands-on presentations and live animals to teach ecology. Summer library programs are free.

Directions: From Houston, take I-10 west to the Beltway 8 Frontage Road exit. Turn left (south) onto the Frontage Road under Beltway 8. Turn right onto Memorial Dr. and go 0.25 mile to Rustling Pines subdivision. Turn left onto Wilchester Blvd. The sanctuary is the second property on the left at 440 Wilchester. The website includes a printable map.

GPS Coordinates: Latitude: 29° 46.288´ N   Longitude: 95° 34.215´ W

The log cabin at Edith L. Moore Nature Sanctuary

Sims Bayou Urban Nature Center

3997 River Dr., Houston, TX 77017

Owner: Houston Audubon Society   **Size:** about 1 acre

Contacts: Phone 713-640-2407; E-mail maweber@houstonaudubon.org

Website: http://www.houstonaudubon.org/default.aspx?MenuItemID=484

Natural Region: Gulf Coast Prairies & Marshes

Major Ecosystem(s): Sims Bayou; former coastal prairie

Overview: The headquarters of the Houston Audubon Society Education Department, SBUNC is located in historic Park Place on the original channel of Sims Bayou, which flows northeast into Buffalo Bayou (the Houston Ship Channel). Facilities include a log cabin, nature store, barn, gazebo, gardens, pond with native plants, boat dock, and seasonal wetland trails.

SBUNC is open to the public by appointment only. Groups must schedule tours and classes in advance.

Fun for Kids: Summer day camps for ages 5–12 are offered. The Bayou Buddies preschooler class is on Fridays. Badge workshops for Girl Scouts and Brownies are offered.

Family Fun: The Family Nature Explore Club offers monthly Saturday excursions for families.

Educational: A variety of programs are offered including teacher workshops, field trips, summer day camps, school programs and outreach, scouting programs, and community outreach (emphasizing birds).

Flying WILD Workshops for teachers provide resources for environmental educators and CPE credits.

Directions: From Houston, go south on I-45 and take the Howard/Bellfort exit (# 38B). Make a U-turn under the freeway onto the northbound feeder. Turn right just before the Shell gas station onto River Dr. Go 0.5 mile to SBUNC on the right next to the tennis courts. The website includes a printable map with directions.

GPS Coordinates: Latitude: 29° 41.198´ N   Longitude: 95° 16.349´ W

The Sims Bayou Urban Nature Center

87 The Children's Museum of Houston's EcoStation

1500 Binz St., Houston, TX 77004

Owner: Children's Museum of Houston

Contacts: Phone 713-522-1138; E-mail form on website

Website: www.cmhouston.org

Natural Region: Gulf Coast Prairies & Marshes

Major Ecosystem(s): Urban

Overview: EcoStation is an interactive indoor/outdoor environmental exhibit where visitors engage in ecological studies and explore environmental issues by visiting a native plant garden, woodland area, pond, and research pavilion. Visitors can participate in diverse hands-on activities such as bird-watching, scavenger hunts, pond study, leaf rubbings, animal track identification, Tree Stump Amphitheater talks, etc. Weekly changing programming includes topics such as nature journals, water quality testing, recycling, natural cycles, soil characteristics, animal behaviors, home environmental awareness inventory logs, bird feeders, etc.

Almost all of EcoStation is solar powered. There is an exhibit activity about solar power and its use by the museum.

Fun for Kids: There are hands-on activities like scavenger hunts and leaf rubbings.

Family Fun: Free weekly Family Nights are on Thursdays. Occasional WonderWeeks with environmental themes are offered.

Educational: School field experiences are for grades K–5. Classroom curricula on 10 topics dealing with plants, birds, insects, and Houston's ecosystems and environmental issues are available online, and are aligned with state education standards. Teacher workshops for CPE credit are offered.

Directions: From downtown Houston, take US 59 South or I-45 South to 288 South. Exit on Binz St and stay on the feeder. Turn right on Binz. CMH is 7 blocks on the left. Or, go south on Fannin St. and turn left on Binz. CMH is 4 blocks on the right. The website includes a printable map.

GPS Coordinates: Latitude: 29° 43.341' N   Longitude: 95° 23.190' W

The Children's Museum of Houston

⠿ Hana & Arthur Ginzbarg Nature Discovery Center

7112 Newcastle St., Bellaire, TX 77401

Owner: Nature Discovery Center, Inc.   **Size:** 4 acres

Contacts: Phone 713-667-6550; Fax 713-667-7654;
E-mail mail@naturediscoverycenter.org

Website: www.naturediscoverycenter.org

Natural Region: Gulf Coast Prairies & Marshes

Major Ecosystem(s): Urban forest, mixed pine-hardwood

Overview: HAGNDC is in Russ Pitman Park in Bellaire. The Discovery Rooms are in the renovated, historic Henshaw House. There are covered picnic tables in the pavilion behind the center.

Facilities include a playground, herb garden, prairie garden, trails, and a small wetland "bog." The urban forest consists of trees such as oak and pecan.

Fun for Kids: Summer science camps are for ages 5–10. School holiday camps are offered. There is a free story time for preschoolers. Scouting programs are available.

Family Fun: The Discovery Rooms are open and free to individuals and families. Interactive exhibits and 23 Discovery Boxes provide hands-on experience. Adult lectures and nature field trips as well as family friendly events are offered.

Educational: School field trips are based on the state-aligned Nature at Your Doorstep teachers' manual intended for grades pre-K–5.

The outreach program can bring interactive programs and live animals to your classroom, and Traveling Science Exhibits can be rented by the month. Teacher training workshops offer CPE credit, and other teacher resources are available.

Directions: From I-610 West going south, take the Bellaire Blvd. exit, go to the stop light at Newcastle St., continue about 0.4 mile, then turn right into the parking lot at mailbox 7112. The website includes a printable map.

GPS Coordinates: Latitude: 29° 42.029' N   Longitude: 95° 27.090' W

The Hana and Arthur Ginzbarg Nature Discovery Center

Live animals inside the Nature Discovery Center

89 Houston Arboretum & Nature Center

4501 Woodway Dr., Houston, TX 77024

Owner: HANC   **Size:** 155 acres

Contacts: Phone 713-681-8433; Fax 713-681-1191; E-mail arbor@houstonarboretum.org

Website: www.houstonarboretum.org

Natural Region: Gulf Coast Prairies & Marshes

Major Ecosystem(s): Buffalo Bayou frontage and floodplain

Overview: Located on the west edge of Memorial Park, HANC has frontage on Buffalo Bayou. It includes mixed pine-hardwood forest, demonstration grassland, and several excavated ponds. There are 5 miles of walking trails, an interpretive center with a Discovery Room featuring hands-on activities and exhibits, a nature gift shop, and classrooms. The Palmetto Multi-sensory Trail was designed to serve the visually impaired.

There is no admission fee.

Fun for Kids: Programs include summer Nature Discovery Camps; as well as winter and spring break camps. There are programs for scouts and homeschool classes.

Family Fun: Family oriented programs include nature and ecology classes for preschoolers through age 12.

Educational: A wide range of K–12 school programs emphasizing hands-on outdoor guided field experiences aligned with state education standards is offered. Discovery Room activities and exhibits reinforce the field experiences. A wide variety of professional development courses (for CPE credit), workshops, and teacher resources are available. School outreach programs are for grades K–5.

Directions: Located on the west side of Houston, south of I-10 and about 0.125 mile east of the I-610 Loop West on Woodway Dr. This is the southwest corner of Memorial Park. The website includes a printable map.

GPS Coordinates: Latitude: 29° 46.048´ N   Longitude: 95° 27.148´ W

The Houston Arboretum & Nature Center VC

A yellow crowned night heron at HANC

90 Armand Bayou Nature Center

8500 Bay Area Blvd., Pasadena, TX 77507

Owner: ABNC, Inc.   **Size:** 2,500 acres

Contacts: Phone 281-474-2551; Fax 281-474-2552; E-mail abnc@abnc.org

Website: http://abnc.org/

Natural Region: Gulf Coast Prairies & Marshes

Major Ecosystem(s): Armand Bayou (tidal); coastal prairie, marshes, riparian hardwoods

Overview: ABNC is one of the largest urban wildlife refuges in the U.S. In addition to the tidal bayou, other habitats include remnant coastal prairie and fresh marsh, riparian hardwoods, and restored saltmarshes. Facilities include an education center, a teaching boardwalk through the forest and marshes, live animal displays, educational signage, bison and prairie platforms, butterfly gardens, and an 1800s farm site.

Over 5 miles of trails traverse forest, prairie, marsh, and bayou habitats once common in the Houston/Galveston area. Armand Bayou is one of the last remaining unchannelized bayous in the Houston area.

Fun for Kids: Outdoor nature day camps (EcoCamp) are held in both summer and over winter school breaks to provide interactive experiential learning for 4- to 13-year-olds. The education center contains displays of live reptiles, fish, amphibians, and touch tables. A 600-foot "teaching boardwalk" crosses a pond with wetland wildlife.

Family Fun: Special events include Earth Day in April, Creepy Crawlers in October, and Martyn Farm Harvest Festival in November. There are weekend classes for families and children, scouting programs, adult nature-oriented certification programs, guided trail hikes, animal demonstrations, craft demonstrations, and canoe and pontoon boat trips. These guided EcoExplorations provide public access to the habitats and ecology of the site. The Armand Bayou Paddle Trail can be accessed from the center.

Educational: EcoEducation programs for school groups on various natural science or historical subjects are aligned with state education standards. Local gifted and talented classes have regular sessions at ABNC. An outreach program is delivered by staff and trained volunteers. Teacher resources and workshops for CPE credit are available.

Directions: From Houston, go south on I-45 and exit onto Bay Area Blvd. Go east 7 miles just past Bay Area Park to the entrance. The website includes a link to a printable map.

GPS Coordinates: Latitude: 29° 35.907' N   Longitude: 95° 04.485' W

The Education Center at Armand Bayou Nature Center

The teaching boardwalk at Armand Bayou Nature Center

91 Eddie V. Gray Wetlands Education & Recreation Center

1724 Market St., Baytown, TX 77520

Owner: City of Baytown   **Size:** 6 acres

Contacts: Phone 281-420-7128; Fax 281-420-7142; E-mail tracey.prothro@ baytown.org

Website: www.baytown.org/content/eddie-v-gray-wetlands-center

Natural Region: Gulf Coast Prairies & Marshes

Major Ecosystem(s): Galveston Bay estuary; Goose Creek (tidal)

Overview: EVG Center, on the bank of Goose Creek, features a large exhibit hall with a Wetlands Ecology Learning Trail, taxidermy exhibits, Nature Discovery Room, Gator World with live alligators, Wetlands Clean the Water marsh model, Coastal Connection touch tank, a working honeybee hive, and aquaria and terraria. The science lab has microscopes for viewing small marsh organisms. There is a boat dock, floating dock, and constructed wetland on Goose Creek.

Fun for Kids: The Wade Into Wetlands Summer Science Camp is for grades 1–10. Ten weeks of week-long camps focus on topics such as fishing, birding, reptiles, adaptations, geology, oceanography, and nature art. Scouting badges can be earned during camps or at customized workshops. Gator Tales is a free preschool story and activity hour on Wednesday mornings during summer and winter.

Family Fun: Visitors may take a free, self-guided tour of EVG. Boater safety and hunter education courses are offered occasionally.

Educational: Guided field trips for K–12 students include Wetlands Ecology and Liquid Science programs. These programs include state-aligned instruction at EVG as well as outdoor hands-on activities at EVG's partner facility, the Baytown Nature Center. The Wetlands Ecology Program focuses on the importance of wetlands ecosystems. The Liquid Science program focuses on the hydrologic cycle, watersheds, and human impacts on aquatic systems. Additional programs can be tailored to meet specific requests. The Wetlands Wagon Outreach Program to schools (grades pre-K–8), libraries, clubs, and businesses educates about wetlands. EVG staff travels to fairs, festivals, and conferences offering education on local issues.

Directions: From Houston, take I-10 east to Spur 330 exit. Turn south on 330 (Decker Dr.) and go about 4 miles. Cross under TX 146 and follow the curve to the right, after which Decker Dr. becomes Market St. EVG is about another

0.5 mile on the right across from Lee High School. The website includes a printable map.

GPS Coordinates: Latitude: 29° 43.949' N   Longitude: 94° 59.090' W

The Eddie V. Gray Wetlands Education & Recreation Center

An Eddie V. Gray wetland lab with microscopes

The Eddie V. Gray "Wetlands Clean the Water" marsh model

92 Baytown Nature Center

6213 Bayway Dr., Baytown, TX 77520

Owner: City of Baytown   **Size:** 420 acres

Contacts: Phone 281-424-9198; Fax 281-420-7142; E-mail tracey.prothro@ baytown.org

Website: <www.baytown.org/content/baytown-nature-center>

Natural Region: Gulf Coast Prairies & Marshes

Major Ecosystem(s): Galveston Bay estuary; San Jacinto River (tidal); constructed freshwater wetlands

Overview: This site is the outdoor classroom for the Eddie V. Gray Wetlands Center, as well as a recreational public park. It is on the San Jacinto River, about 4 miles from EVG. It has constructed freshwater wetlands on an area that was once a subdivision that was flooded due to land subsidence caused by excessive pumping of fresh groundwater.

Facilities include four fishing piers, picnic sites, a butterfly garden, walking trails, an education stage, 2 scenic pavilions, bird-watching blinds, and a children's nature discovery playground. Habitats also include upland hardwood trees and tidal marsh. The site provides habitats for 317 species of resident and migratory birds, and is designated by the American Bird Conservancy as a nationally important area.

Fun for Kids: The Children's Nature Discovery Area offers activities with nature themes to young children. Tyke Hike is a free preschool story and activity hour on Friday mornings during the fall and spring. The area is used by scout groups for campouts and badge workshops.

Family Fun: The Nurture Nature Series is on the first Saturday of every month. Topics cover nature education on fishing, kayaking, butterflies, reptiles, and wildlife rehabilitation. The program is free with paid park entry. The Nurture Nature Festival (first Saturday in November) features guest speakers, booths, and activities for kids. BNC is used for both education and recreation. The public uses the area for picnics, fishing, and bird-watching.

Educational: EVG utilizes the area as an outdoor classroom for its Wetlands Ecology and Liquid Science Programs. These are guided field trips with state-aligned lessons and resources. BNC also offers the Back to the Bay Program for freshman high school biology students. The program focuses on water quality and habitat conditions in Galveston Bay.

Directions: From Houston, take I-10 east to Spur 330 exit. Turn south on 330 (Decker Dr.). Take the Bayway Dr. exit and turn right. Go about 2 miles on Bayway. BNC will be on the right. The website includes a printable map.

GPS Coordinates: Latitude: 29° 45.300ʹ N   Longitude: 95° 02.140ʹ W

The Baytown Nature Center VC

The Children's Nature Discovery Area at the Baytown Nature Center

93 Artist Boat

2415 Avenue K, Galveston, TX 77550

Owner: Artist Boat, Inc.

Contacts: Phone 409-770-0722; E-mail info@artistboat.org

Website: www.artistboat.org

Natural Region: Gulf Coast Prairies & Marshes

Major Ecosystem(s): Galveston Bay and estuary; Gulf of Mexico

Overview: Artist Boat is an unusual, if not unique, program in Texas dedicated to promoting awareness and preservation of coastal margins and the marine environment. Eco-Art programs combine the arts and sciences to promote exploration and appreciation of coastal and marine habitats. The administrative office at Avenue K in Galveston has a studio for completing large-scale public art, and a large yard with three fleets of kayaks (accommodating 75 youth a day) and trailers for restoring habitats in the coastal zone. Eco-Art programs are primarily delivered at schools and the natural sites where paddling, vessel, and walking adventures take place.

Natural sites include Armand Bayou, Christmas Bay, Drum Bay, Galveston Island State Park, Galveston and Houston Ship Channels, San Jacinto State Historical Park, Smith Point, Trinity River, and cypress swamps on the Trinity.

Fun for Kids: See everything below.

Family Fun: Eco-Art public kayak adventure tours and Habitat Restoration Adventure Program outings are offered.

Educational: Youth Eco-Art Workshops are delivered to students at the school before Eco-Art Adventures. Two-hour workshops include hands-on activities about the ecology, economy, and history of the Galveston Bay system and the Gulf of Mexico. The use of art to interpret nature is demonstrated and applied. Youth Eco-Art Adventures (kayak, vessel, or on foot) are student group field trips that include hands-on outdoor environmental education activities such as paddling and safety lessons, birding, watercolor painting, study of the local ecology, and expanded science activities for walking- and vessel-based programs. Programs are aligned with state education standards and are available for grades K–12 depending upon group size and type of trip. Pre- and post-class curriculum lesson plans are available online.

Professional development opportunities include the Coastal Waters Institute, a 5-day summer hands-on field- and classroom-based course focusing on the Galveston Bay watershed. This program is for seventh and eighth grade teachers and offers CPE credit and a curriculum aligned with state standards. Environmental education grant writing assistance for schools is available, as is the development and writing of place-based and experiential learning curricula.

Directions: Programs are delivered at schools or at the natural sites where field experiences and habitat restoration take place.

GPS Coordinates (Office): Latitude: 29° 17.918΄ N   Longitude: 94° 47.603΄ W

The Artist Boat headquarters in Galveston

Kayaks at Artist Boat headquarters

Waterborne Education Center

509 Washington Ave. (P.O. Box 9), Anahuac, TX 77514

Owner: WEC

Contacts: Phone 409-656-4135; Fax 409-267-3547; E-mail mailto:CatherineWilliams@ChambersRecoveryTeam.org

Website: http://www.txwaterborne.org (under development as of November 2013)

Natural Region: Gulf Coast Prairies & Marshes

Major Ecosystem(s): Galveston Bay estuary; Trinity River

Overview: The WEC provides hands-on waterborne education services designed to foster appreciation and stewardship of coastal resources by teaching about the ecology, history, and economic productivity of the Texas coast.

Field labs are conducted aboard a 45-foot renovated Coast Guard buoy tender. The vessel carries 25 participants and has a lab below deck and a gangplank to permit unloading of passengers in the wetlands.

Fun for Kids: Boat rides and wading in the wetlands.

Educational: A variety of field labs emphasizes coastal ecology, history, and economics. Hands-on activities include seining, water quality testing, environmental stewardship, etc. Instruction is aligned with state education standards for grades 5–12 and also for college level students. The WEC is a certified provider of CPE credit for teachers through teacher training workshops.

Field labs are conducted in the Galveston Bay estuary and the Trinity River and its delta. Partial scholarships may be available to non-profit groups.

Directions: From I-10 between Houston and Beaumont, take the Anahuac/ Liberty exit. Take FM 563 for 6 miles to Anahuac. Cross the canal and come to the 4-way stop. Make a right turn onto Miller St. (Hwy 61). Turn left on Washington Ave. The WEC office is in the Sandlin Bldg. across from the Chambers County Courthouse. The website includes a link to a printable map.

GPS Coordinates: Latitude: 29° 46.095´ N   Longitude: 94° 41.052´ W

A smaller WEC teaching boat

The teaching vessel *Moss Bluff* at the Waterborne Education Center

Anahuac National Wildlife Refuge

4017 FM 563, Anahuac, TX 77514

Owner: U.S. Fish & Wildlife Service   **Size:** 34,000 acres

Contacts: Phone 409-267-3337; Fax 409-267-4314; E-mail mailto:maria_vielma@fws.govm

Website: www.fws.gov/refuge/Anahuac/

Natural Region: Gulf Coast Prairies & Marshes

Major Ecosystem(s): East Galveston Bay; coastal prairie, tidal and fresh marshes

Overview: The main refuge is about a 1.5 hour drive east of Houston on East Galveston Bay. Several bayous meander across the coastal prairie, creating wetlands ranging from freshwater to saltmarshes. The wetlands support large numbers of wintering waterfowl as well as resident wildlife. The trees along some bayous provide migration habitat for songbirds, especially in spring. There is no drinking water available on the refuge and don't forget your mosquito repellent.

The headquarters and VC complex is north of the town of Anahuac on FM 563 about 2.5 miles south of I-10. The building has LEED® gold status and features solar voltaic panels and a rainwater collection system. It also has a boardwalk through the cypress swamp to Lake Anahuac. There is an interactive virtual airboat ride through the marsh inside the VC. This complex is 15 miles from the main refuge.

Fun for Kids: At the main refuge entrance is a Visitor Information Station that includes a nature store, interpretive exhibits, and an information desk. There is a butterfly and hummingbird habitat/trail at the VC.

Family Fun: A paved 2.5 mile auto tour loop features a boardwalk and overlook. The Skillern Tract, 7 miles east of the main entrance on FM 1985, features a 1-mile trail along East Bay Bayou and a covered overlook. There are special annual events like Gator Fest, Rice Fest, Anahuac Wildlife Expo, and Family Fishing Day.

Educational: The refuge hosts, with the Friends of Anahuac Refuge, an outdoor education program that is free to schools and organizations. Classes that are held outdoors are 1 to 1.5 hours long and are designed for K–fifth grades. Classes are hands-on and cover a wide variety of subjects such as wetlands, reptiles, insects, food webs, etc. Reservations are required. An annual Wild Things! reading program for local fifth graders Is offered.

Directions: Main Refuge—From Houston, take I-10 east to Exit 812 (TX 61). Go south on TX 61 about 4 miles to the stop sign. Go through the stop sign. The road becomes Hwy 562. Go 8.5 miles on 562 to the fork in the road. Turn left onto FM 1985 and go 4 miles to the refuge entrance. The website includes a printable map.

GPS Coordinates: Latitude: 29° 39.507 N   Longitude: 94° 32.814 W

Headquarters/VC Complex—From Houston, take I-10 east to Exit 810 (FM 563). Go south about 2.5 miles on FM 563 to the headquarters. The website includes a printable map.

GPS Coordinates: Latitude: 29° 49.336 N   Longitude: 94° 39.853 W

The Anahuac National Wildlife Refuge VC

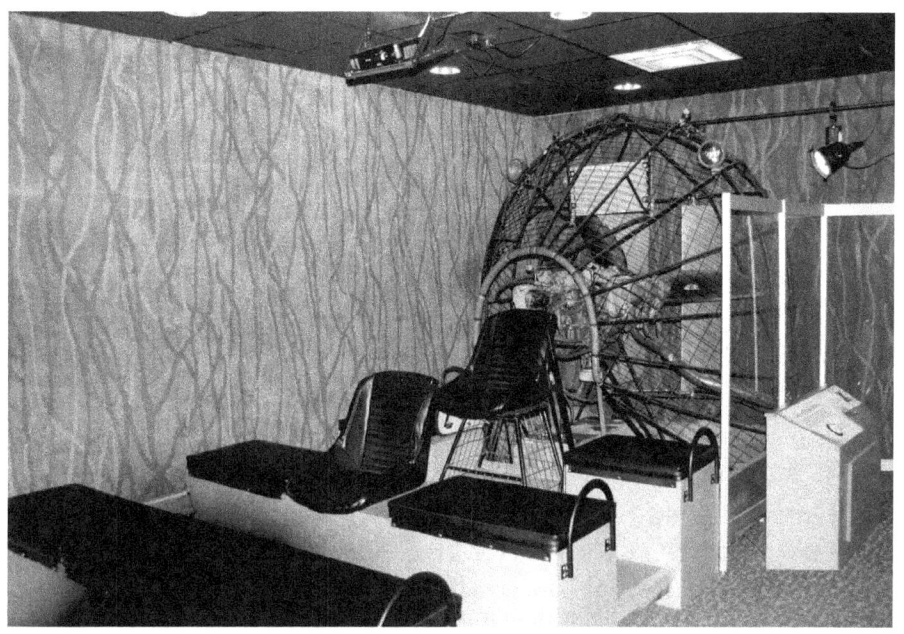

The simulated airboat ride in the VC at Anahuac NWR

A boardwalk in the cypress swamp at Anahuac NWR

96 Shangri La Botanical Gardens & Nature Center

2111 West Park Ave., Orange, TX 77630

Owner: Nelda C. and H. J. Lutcher Stark Foundation   **Size:** 262 acres

Contacts: Phone 409-670-9113; Fax 409-670-9341;
E-mail info@shangrilagardens.org

Website: http://starkculturalvenues.org/shangrilagardens/

Natural Region: Gulf Coast Prairies & Marshes

Major Ecosystem(s): Adams Bayou/Sabine River; cypress-tupelo swamp

Overview: The formal gardens contain over 300 plant species. The Orientation Center includes an Exhibit Hall, Discovery Theatre, interactive Children's Garden, Water Demo Garden, café, and garden store. The Nature Center has a hands-on exhibit called the Nature Discovery Center, an interactive laboratory, and two outdoor Outposts adjacent to a beaver pond. Access to these Outposts is via a teacher-guided tour aboard electric pontoon boats. Each Outpost is adjacent to a cypress swamp, grassland, and upland forest.

Shangri La is LEED® platinum-certified and a U.S. Green Building Council Top Ten Green Project.

Fun for Kids: The EcoRanger program's art and nature summer camps provide hands-on learning in natural environments for grades 3–9.

Family Fun: There are weekly and monthly events, like the Saturday Adventure Series and Up Close with Nature, and annual events like Eco-Fest, Earth Week Celebration, and Autumn Fair.

Educational: A school tour program provides environmental education for students throughout the region. The tours may include taking boats and boardwalks to the classrooms. Students may sample and test water quality in the Water Demo Garden. Options include naturalist-guided school programs, teacher-guided explorer programs, and outreach programs where a naturalist comes to the classroom. Naturalist-guided programs are aligned with state standards for grades pre-K–8. Free teacher workshops in natural and physical sciences offer CPE credit.

School tour and outreach programs are free to schools in Orange County. There is free busing for schools in Orange County.

Directions: From I-10 in Orange, take Exit 877 (Hwy 87/16th St.). Follow the feeder road and turn right onto 16th St. Go 2 miles to West Park Ave. Turn right and go just under 0.5 mile to the main gate on the left. General parking is across the street on the right. The website includes a printable map.

GPS Coordinates: Latitude: 30°06.237ʹ N   Longitude: 93°45.146ʹ W

The Shangri La Botanical Gardens & Nature Center

One of the electric pontoon boats at Shangri La

The Discovery Theatre at Shangri La

References/Suggested Reading

Brown, L. R. 2011. World on the Edge: How to Prevent Environmental and Economic Collapse. W. W. Norton and Co., New York, NY.

Brune, G. 2002. *Springs of Texas, Second Edition*. Texas A & M Press, College Station, TX.

Diamond, J. 2011. *Collapse: How Societies Choose to Fail or Succeed*. Penguin Books, New York, NY.

Flannery, T. F. 2005. *The Weather Makers: How Man Is Changing the Climate and What It Means for Life on Earth*. Atlantic Monthly Press, New York, NY.

Graham, G. L. 1992. *Texas Wildlife Viewing Guide*. Falcon Press Publishing Co., Inc. Helena and Billings, MT.

LBJ School of Public Affairs. 1978. *Preserving Texas' Natural Heritage. Policy Research Project Report 31*. Univ. of Texas, Austin, TX.

Louv, R. 2005. *Last Child in the Woods: Saving Our Children from Nature-Deficit Disorder*. Algonquin Books, Chapel Hill, NC.

McMahan, C. A., R. G. Frye, and K. L. Brown. 1984. *The Vegetation Types of Texas*. Texas Parks and Wildlife Dept., Austin, TX.

Moulton, D. W. and J. S. Jacob. 2000. *Texas Coastal Wetlands Guidebook*. Texas Sea Grant College Program, Bryan, TX.

Moulton, D. W., L. D. McKinney, and D. L. Buzan. 2004. *Texas Coastal Ecosystems: Past, Present and Future*. Texas Sea Grant College Program, College Station, TX.

Schmidly, D. J. 2002. *Texas Natural History: A Century of Change*. Texas Tech Univ. Press, Lubbock, TX.

Spearing, D. 1991. *Roadside Geology of Texas*. Mountain Press Publishing Co., Missoula, MT.

Appendix—An Environmental Primer

The following topics represent a consensus of the world's environmental scientists concerning the major environmental issues confronting us all. All of these issues are inextricably interrelated.

Human Population

This issue is the dominant influence driving all the others. The Earth is a finite space with finite resources available to support all living things. The planet's ability to absorb and process waste and pollution is also finite.

The U.S. Census Bureau provides the most reliable estimates and projections for U.S. and world population. The 2012 world population exceeded 7,042,000,000. By 2050, this number is projected to exceed 9,400,000,000.[1] The good news is the rate of population growth is slowing and the total is expected to level off between 9 and 11 billion by 2100. The question is what kind of lifestyle can the planet support for that many people? Certainly, people who live as high on the hog as we in the U.S. do will be compelled to make significant lifestyle changes.

The 2012 population of the U.S. was about 315 million. By 2050, the number is projected to be about 439 million.[2] The population of Texas is now about 26 million. By 2040, the number is projected to be almost 36 million, about as many as now live in California.[3]

All these people will consume ever-increasing quantities of natural resources such as land, water, food, and energy. At the other end of consumption will be ever-increasing amounts of waste and pollution. As the bill for exceeding the carrying capacity of the planet starts to come due, the tragic consequences may include mass migrations, war, famine, and disease precipitated by ecosystem collapses. There are places in the world, for example in parts of Africa, where we have already glimpsed what can happen when the demand for resources exceeds the available supplies. The underdeveloped (poor) areas of the world will suffer the worst because they can't afford to import resources from other nations.

[1] www.census.gov/population/international/data/idb/informationGateway.php

[2] www.census.gov/population/projections/

[3] txsdc.utsa.edu/Data/TPEPP/Projections/Index.aspx

Ecological Footprint

The ecological footprint is a method to measure human demands on the Earth's ecosystems. It estimates the area of biologically productive land and ocean required to supply the resources human populations consume, and to assimilate associated waste. Footprints can be calculated for individuals, businesses, cities, nations, and the whole world.

According to the Global Footprint Network, if current population and consumption trends continue, by the 2030s we will need two Earths to support us all.[1] It now takes the Earth one year and six months to regenerate the resources we use in one year and to absorb our waste. If everyone lived the lifestyle of the average American, we would need five Earths! Obviously, this situation is not sustainable.

Want to calculate your own ecological footprint? There are several calculators you can access on the Internet.[2,3] Want to see how much pollution your car produces in a year? There is a website for that too.[4]

There are several websites that can assist a person, family, business, or city shrink their ecological footprint through green living. I suggest the EPA's.[5]

[1] www.footprintnetwork.org/en/index.php/GFN/page/basics_introduction/

[2] myfootprint.org/

[3] www.earthday.org/footprint-calculator

[4] autos.yahoo.com/green_center-article_1/

[5] www2.epa.gov/learn-issues/learn-about-green-living

Global Warming & Climate Change

The Earth has been in an interglacial (between Ice Ages) warming period since the end of the last Ice Age, about 10 thousand years ago. Warming periods occur after every Ice Age. Our problem is that human activities that produce carbon dioxide and other greenhouse gases are accelerating the Earth's warming. This is causing problems such as rapid sea level rise, droughts, more frequent and powerful storms, more frequent and severe wildfires, and instability in ecosystems around the globe.

The Intergovernmental Panel on Climate Change (IPCC) was established in 1988 by the United Nations Environment Program and the World Meteorological Organization.[1] Its purpose is to study what is known about climate change and its potential environmental and socio-economic impacts. Thousands of scientists from 195 nations contribute to the work on a voluntary basis. The work of the IPCC leaves no doubt that the planet is warming and climate changes are occurring. There is also no doubt that the production of carbon dioxide and other greenhouse gases, primarily by the burning of coal, oil, and other fossil fuels, is speeding the warming process. The IPCC also studies methods whereby humans can mitigate and/or adapt to ongoing climate change around the world.

The purpose of the nonprofit group Citizens Climate Lobby is to create the political will for a stable climate and a livable world.[2] Dr. James Hansen, director of NASA's Goddard Institute for Space Studies and one of the world's leading climate scientists, has said of this organization, "If you want to join the fight to save the planet, to save creation for your grandchildren, there is no more effective step you could take than becoming an active member of this group."

Other websites you can visit to learn more about global warming and climate change are those of the EPA and the Union of Concerned Scientists.[3, 4]

[1] www.ipcc.ch/index.htm

[2] www.citizensclimatelobby.org

[3] www.epa.gov/climatechange/

[4] www.ucsusa.org/global_warming/

Renewable Energy

The website of the U.S. Energy Information Administration has a section entitled Energy and the Environment Explained.[1] This site includes information on renewable energy sources which, unlike fossil fuels, are sustainable. Renewable sources such as solar, wind, geothermal, and hydropower are also clean (green).

The EPA and Union of Concerned Scientists have websites that discuss in detail the sources and advantages of renewable energy.[2, 3] The Public Utilities Commission of Texas maintains a website that enables energy customers in Texas to shop online for providers of clean energy.[4]

Unlike fossil fuels, green power sources don't produce greenhouse gases and other toxics and pollutants.

[1] www.eia.gov/environment/

[2] www.epa.gov/greenpower/pubs/gplocator.htm

[3] www.ucsusa.org/clean_energy/

[4] www.powertochoose.org/en-us/

Pollution & Toxic Chemicals

Burning fossil fuels produces pollutants and toxins in addition to greenhouse gases. Transportation, agriculture, industry, businesses, and individuals introduce many pesticides, chemicals, and toxins into our environment. The EPA maintains a website where you can find out more about the issues caused by these materials.[1]

Find out more about air pollutants in your environment at websites of the EPA and the Texas Commission on Environmental Quality.[2,3] These agencies also have websites where you can find out about pollutants in your water.[4,5] The EPA has a site where you can learn about the health effects caused by pollutants in the environment around us and what you can do to ensure health and safety.[6]

[1] www2.epa.gov/learn-issues/learn-about-chemicals-and-toxics

[2] www2.epa.gov/learn-issues/learn-about-air

[3] www.tceq.texas.gov/agency/air_main.html

[4] www2.epa.gov/learn-issues/learn-about-water

[5] www.tceq.texas.gov/agency/water_main.html

[6] www2.epa.gov/learn-issues/learn-about-health-and-safety

Endangered Species

Major mass extinction events have occurred at least five times in the last 540 million years; the most recent event occurring about 65.5 million years ago. The causes of these events are varied and not completely understood. The most recent event apparently involved an asteroid striking the Earth.

Because the normal background rate of extinction is rising sharply, many scientists think a mass extinction event may now be underway. If so, the cause is almost certainly extensive global habitat destruction and alteration caused by humans. As humans use more and more of the Earth's limited natural resources there is less and less available to support all other species. The loss of habitats combined with the loss of species may eventually cause ecosystem collapses. This would certainly be accompanied by the collapse of human economies at various levels. Some of the potential human consequences were mentioned above.

The International Union for Conservation of Nature (IUCN) maintains a Red List of Threatened Species that is the most authoritative accounting of threatened and endangered plants and animals around the globe.[1] The U.S. Fish and Wildlife Service has responsibility for most of the threatened and endangered species in the U.S.[2] The Texas Parks and Wildlife Department maintains a listing of rare and endangered species in Texas.[3]

[1] www.iucnredlist.org/

[2] www.fws.gov/endangered/

[3] www.tpwd.state.tx.us/ (search rare and endangered species)

The Economy vs. the Environment

If you think protecting our environment hinders economic development, I urge you to explore the websites mentioned below. Many of the world's largest multi-national corporations openly subscribe to the philosophy that the long-term sustainability of their industries is directly dependent on sustainable environments.

The World Business Council for Sustainable Development consists of 200 member corporations from around the globe.[1] Its purpose is to galvanize the global business community to create a sustainable future for business, society, and the environment. In the long run, protecting the environment is good for business!

The Worldwatch Institute works to accelerate the transition to a sustainable world that meets human needs. The organization's Sustainable Prosperity Project looks at current trends in global economics and sustainability, and charts a path for reforming economic institutions to promote both ecological health and human prosperity.[2]

The Earth Policy Institute tracks twelve trends they call Eco-Economy Indicators to measure progress in building a sustainable economy. Their website presents interesting data and discussion for these trends.[3]

You may have noticed the term "economic growth" being replaced by the term "economic development." Unlimited growth of an economy, or anything else, is impossible! Economic development, on the other hand, suggests continuous change on a sustainable basis. For example, the transition from fossil fuels to renewable energy sources would generate entire new industries. Predictably, this prospect does not seem to appeal to the coal and petroleum industries. Likewise, the electric generation industry has not embraced the transition to renewable energy sources. Some may question whether this may relate to their inability to meter the sunlight that hits your roof. These industries are very profitable and they use their wealth to lobby our elected representatives. The result has been the general lack of interest our government has shown in assisting the inevitable transition to clean energy.

In the long run, the sustainability of these industries will require visionary leadership that not only embraces but invests in the changes that must come. It would be helpful if our government would do more to encourage and assist in this transition.

[1] www.wbcsd.org

[2] www.worldwatch.org/sustainable-prosperity-project

[3] www.earth-policy.org/publications/C39

Politics and the Environment

Concern for our environment should and sometimes does transcend politics. For example, not all Republicans subscribe to the "drill baby, drill" philosophy of natural resources management. ConservAmerica, formerly known as Republicans for Environmental Protection, aims to resurrect the GOP's great conservation tradition and to restore natural resource conservation and sound environmental protection as fundamental elements of the Republican Party's vision for America. Their motto is "Conservation is Conservative!"® and their website is entitled "Growing a Greener GOP From the Ground Up."[1]

[1] conservamerica.org

Sustainable Life—The Big Picture

You may have noticed that the word sustainable, and its variations, was repeated perhaps too often in this book. Life first appeared on Earth about 3,500,000,000 years ago and has persisted ever since. Why has life on Earth been so remarkably sustainable? It's because natural selection (environmental influences), working through the process of evolution (a word meaning change), causes living organisms and ecosystems to obey the unbreakable laws of conservation of matter and energy. As Earth's environments change over time, evolution causes species and ecosystems to change as well, so the laws of nature remain unbroken and life continues.

Matter, such as the elements carbon, oxygen, nitrogen, etc., can be recycled and used again and again by living organisms. Decomposers, mainly bacteria and fungi, have evolved to be highly efficient in recycling the matter needed to sustain life. Energy, on the other hand, can't be recycled. A continuous source of outside energy is needed to power life. For the great majority of living things that energy source is our Sun. Photosynthesizing organisms, mainly green plants and algae, have evolved a very efficient chemical process to convert the energy of sunlight into matter (food) for use by the plants and algae themselves and, through food chains, by almost all animals.

So, the basic principles of life's sustainability are:

- Efficient recycling of matter.
- Use of the Sun for energy.[1]
- Adaptation through change.

We would be well advised to try our best to emulate this model of sustainability that created us and that, so far, has sustained us.

[1] In addition to sunlight, wind and running water (for hydropower) are created by the Sun's energy heating air masses and driving the hydrologic cycle.

Available on Amazon.com as an e-book and in print.

To Purchase Additional Copies of This Book

and to arrange for book signings or speaking events

contact the author:

Dan Moulton
Phone: 972-620-7523
dan_moulton@sbcglobal.net
3764 Chatham Ct. Dr.
Addison, TX 75001

Publisher Contact: Lone Star Productions
Ginnie Bivona 972-671-0002
ginniebivona@sbcglobal.net

www.ingramcontent.com/pod-product-compliance
Lightning Source LLC
Chambersburg PA
CBHW060451290526
45791CB00001B/65